30 Stories
in 30 Years

30 Stories
in 30 Years

Escapes from Death, 11th Hour Deliverances,
Miracles, and other Missionary Adventures

Timothy H. Anderson

Visit Timothy on Facebook: www.facebook.com/ecuadorecho

30 Stories in 30 Years – Timothy H. Anderson

Copyright © 2016

First edition published 2016

Scripture taken from the New King James Version®. Copyright © 1982 by Thomas Nelson. Used by permission. All rights reserved.

Cover Design: Natalia Hawthorne, BookCoverLabs.com

ebook: Icons Vector/Shutterstock

Editor: Heather Thomas

Printed in the United States of America

Aneko Press – *Our Readers Matter*[TM]

www.anekopress.com

Aneko Press, Life Sentence Publishing, and our logos are trademarks of

Life Sentence Publishing, Inc.
203 E. Birch Street
P.O. Box 652
Abbotsford, WI 54405

BIOGRAPHY & AUTOBIOGRAPHY / Religious

Paperback ISBN: 978-1-62245-394-8

eBook ISBN: 978-1-62245-395-5

10   9   8   7   6   5   4   3   2   1

Available where books are sold.

Contents

Foreword

———◇◇◇———

Whis strawberry-blonde hair and freckles from a distance. He
didn't know who I was or that I even existed.

Ten years later in 1982, I met Tim Anderson at a church we
both started attending in December of 1981. Our cell group
numbers were down that night, so they merged the groups. The
discussion question for that night was, "What is God's call for
your life?" We were sitting in a church about thirty minutes
from our home town. We found out that night, we were *both*
from Baldwinsville. We shared with each other how we felt
God's call on our lives to do missions work in Latin America.

In September of 1982, we started dating. We were engaged by
February and married five months later. We left for the mission

field in December of 1987 with three children under three years old. We spent our first year in Costa Rica attending language school. During that time, we learned Spanish and adapted to Latin American customs and culture.

Now, we are approaching our thirty-third year of marriage. Thirty of those have been spent in overseas missions. We have had a "wild ride" serving the Lord. Living in a foreign country, we've been through mudslides, earthquakes, and illness. We've also experience direct threats and danger to our family and as a couple. I'd rather not ponder the reality of what could have happened for any length of time.

Tim is the *real deal.* He's a modern-day Prophet-Evangelist. In the face of spiritual warfare, he endeavors to live a pure and holy life with immeasurable power and a fiery anointing. Satan has attempted, in many ways, to wipe my husband from the face of the earth. He remains only by the mighty hand of God. His life verse is: *The kingdom of heaven suffers violence, and the violent take it by force* (Matthew 11:12).

I stand amazed at the remarkable and innumerable ways Jesus Christ has used my husband to free the captives, heal those in physical and emotional pain, and witness to thousands upon thousands. It has not been "a piece of cake" being married to a modern-day, no-holds-barred follower of Jesus, but the joys and riches we have experienced together have been worth it. You will stand amazed as you join our adventure shared through-out these pages. Thanks for teaming up with us for God's glory and Ecuador's Harvest!

– Debbie Anderson, Ph.D.

Introduction

————————— ✕◇✕ —————————

The Call

My call to serve in foreign missions came in 1981 while I was in a live-in staff position (the Dean of Men) at Syracuse Teen Challenge. The Lord spoke to me as I read my Bible in the South Avenue McDonald's one morning. *By faith, Abraham obeyed when he was called to go out to the place which he would receive as an inheritance. And he went out, not knowing where he was going* (Hebrews 11:8).

I felt like I was struck by lightning. The words seemed to jump off the pages of my Bible. The Holy Spirit spoke to me as clearly and firmly as I had ever heard Him. *You are to identify with Abraham and serve me in a foreign land.* I was overwhelmed, excited, and overjoyed at this new and powerful revelation and direction for my life. God had been preparing my heart for several years prior to coming to Syracuse Teen Challenge in 1979. I listened to Christian radio programs. I read biographies of great Christian lives and heard missionaries speak at church.

Questions flooded my mind. *Is it right for you to continue to stay in the U.S. with so many Gospel churches and ministries when there are people in other lands who have never heard the Gospel even once? Does that seem right to you? Don't they also have the right to hear?* The Holy Spirit was in the process of cultivating the soil of my heart for the mission's call. The questions became a challenge that I was prepared to answer.

At the time of God's calling, I didn't have a specific country in mind. I did feel in my heart that it would be a Spanish-speaking country in South America. These deeply-felt convictions would prove to be true. However, it would be five more years until we were appointed as missionaries by the Assemblies of God. Followed by two more years before we reached the country in which we were to serve.

The Confirmation, the Wedding, and the Release

After I received such a powerful and clear calling from God to serve Him in a foreign land (Hebrews 11:8), I began to study Spanish twice a week with my good friend, Syracuse University Professor, Max Rossi. He and his wife, Olympia, were gracious and loving to me as we met at their house for many months to study Spanish. We shared in wonderful fellowship and stood in awe of what God was doing in our lives.

Six months passed from the time I received the call. I expected to be on my way to the mission field within the year. I thought at least I'd be somewhere other than Syracuse. As I read my Bible during devotions one evening at Teen Challenge, I felt the Lord speak deeply to my heart. *If you have run with the footmen, and they have wearied you, then how can you contend with horses? And if in the land of peace, in which you trusted, they wearied you, then how will you do in the floodplain of the Jordan?* (Jeremiah 12:5).

The Holy Spirit spoke clearly and forcefully to me saying, *Tim, you are not ready to leave yet. Stay where you are, learn and grow. I'll make it clear when you are to leave, and where you are to go.* My heart was crushed. It was God speaking to me. I would never leave without His blessing and His presence going with me. This is what I came to understand as the second part of God's *calling* or God's *vision*. It's known as "The Death of a Vision." It was a painful, yet vital, part of God's plan to deepen His work in me and prepare me for what laid ahead. I had already lived and ministered in Syracuse Teen Challenge for two and a half years, and it would be another two and a half. I also spent an additional three years at the Syracuse Rescue Mission under the director, Clarence Jordan, before I was released to fulfill God's call to be an Assemblies of God foreign missionary.

In the five years after the Word from the book of Jeremiah to wait and serve until His release, I was taken to new and deeper places of prayer, deliverance ministry, and perseverance. My plans were to serve God as a single missionary, but God had other plans, better plans.

In God's sovereignty, I met Joan Gale at the B'ville Diner after a prayer meeting in 1980. She was very sociable and outgoing. I visited her on a regular basis. She read her daughter's letters to me and very much wanted us to meet. At that time, I had no interest in meeting anyone. It was the kingdom that counted and nothing else. I was not interested at all in meeting her daughter, Debbie, and it wouldn't happen while Jo Gale was alive. I stopped going to the St. Mary's Church prayer meetings in 1981. I attended an independent church called Covenant of Salt in Manlius, New York. I didn't see Jo Gale after that.

When Debbie and I met in April of 1982 at Grace Assembly of God on a Wednesday night, I knew there was something special about her. She wrote a poem honoring her mother's life and Christian influence. It was published in our local newspaper, The Messenger. My brother, Rand, read it to me two weeks before I met her.

When we met, I said, "Are you the Debbie Gale who wrote the poem in our local newspaper about your mother?"

She said, "Yes." Then she asked, "Are you the Tim my mother wrote about in her journals and letters to me?"

I said, "I never knew she did that."

Debbie responded, "Your name was mentioned numerous times by my Mom when she wrote to me as well as in her personal journals. I have them. I'll show you."

Wow! This seemed too incredible to happen. So much so, that I saw red flags all over the place. After all, I was a faithful member of the Eunuchs for the Kingdom Club that a bunch of us single guys from the Teen Challenge leadership staff created. I wondered if this was the devil trying to distract me from my calling. That is how I first saw Debbie. Even though she was the prettiest and most vivacious girl I'd ever seen, I knew the devil's trap when I saw it. I wasn't about to be led into the net.

Living and ministering in Teen Challenge was the most demanding and rewarding period of my life. We dealt with many difficult and rebellious young men and the demons that controlled them. Everything was life and death, black or white, right or wrong. No middle ground. No compromise. No giving in to the enemy for even a moment. When Debbie came into the picture, that was my mindset. I was like a steel pole stuck in cement. That year, God broke and humbled my heart to make room for a possible life partner who "happened" to have a missionary call on her life too.

Debbie returned to Texas to finish up her Master's degree in Bilingual Education that summer of 1982. We didn't think much of each other until she returned that fall to live in Syracuse permanently. Early in September, a veteran missionary to Bolivia, Melvin Todd, spoke at Grace Assembly of God. As he preached about missions and the need for laborers. My heart burned with a great desire to pursue the mission's call. Well, lo and behold, who should I see in the church service but Debbie Gale. She was back from Texas. I just *had* to get with her and practice Spanish to prepare for the mission field. She agreed to the Spanish lesson. I suggested we start that afternoon.

Then, when we had our Spanish lesson that afternoon at her apartment, I didn't hear a word she said. I was falling completely in love with her. I was amazed at how fast it was happening. Three days after that Wednesday evening service, we agreed to meet at Denny's Restaurant. I needed to speak to Debbie and express what I was feeling.

As I stirred my coffee about ninety miles per hour, I confessed, "I haven't slept in the past three nights. I believe the Lord … wants us … to *date*."

Debbie kept her poker face as she heard me out. She'd never before heard someone include God in their dating plans. This was all unchartered waters for me too. I lived like a monk in a monastery at Teen Challenge for the four years prior.

How does a Christian navigate the intricacies of a serious relationship with God's blessing? We kept ourselves under strict accountability to the leaders at Grace Assembly, especially one of our deacons there, John Daigle. We agreed to only be together in public places and not spend time alone in her apartment. By the power of God's grace, we were able to keep ourselves from falling into sexual temptation before our wedding day.

Debbie had to give up her free doctoral degree in Educational Administration with Indiana University to marry me and become a missionary. Much to the chagrin and disappointment of her Supervisor, James Mahan, and others, she gave it up. However, after twenty-five years and five children, she earned her Ph.D. on the mission field with Capella University. She finally fulfilled her life-long dream. Debbie is truly one in a million. She gave up her life and dreams only to find that God gave them back and much more. That is why she has been a great missionary and mentor to countless people over the years and the love of my life. We were engaged in February of 1983 and married July 2nd of that same year.

I forgot to mention that during that first chance meeting in the spring of 1982, at Grace Assembly, she shared that she believed it was God's will for her to travel to Latin America and minister to children during her summer vacation months. She was a special education teacher and would be off for ten weeks. She wanted to serve the Lord and use her Spanish as a summer missionary. She already spoke Spanish at an advanced level due to the fact that her master's degree was in Bilingual/Bicultural education. She also taught Mexican-American children in McAllen, Texas, before moving back to Central New York.

Knowing that Debbie also had the call to serve in missions is what clinched the deal for me. Not to mention, she was a very pretty and engaging girl. I had successfully steered my way clear of any sort of serious relationship for several years. I didn't want anything to thwart me from God's purpose for my life. Now, here was someone who shared my passion and calling to Latin America.

Soon after our marriage, we felt the stirring of the Holy Spirit to pursue seriously the call to missions. One evening in the summer of 1985, I read, *Do not remember the former things, nor consider the things of old. Behold, I will do a new thing, now it shall spring forth; shall you not know it? I will even make a road in the wilderness and rivers in the desert* (Isaiah 43:18-19).

The Lord spoke to us, *Now is the time to act. I am with you in this. Now is the time.* That was the third and final step in God's calling, the resurrection of a vision.

This meant I needed to finish the correspondence courses with the Berean School of the Bible for my ordination credentials with the Assemblies of God. Since my degree from Cornell University was a B.S. in Agricultural Economics, I needed to get my Bible School class requirements to be an Assembly of God Minister before becoming a foreign missionary. I was ordained in the spring of 1986. Several months later, Debbie and I received our General Appointment as Assemblies of God Foreign Missionaries.

During those last six months before our missionary appointment, we read the well-documented missionary story, *Through Gates of Splendor*, by Elisabeth Elliot. She was the wife and widow of the late Jim Elliot who, along with four other missionaries, was killed by the Auca Indians in Ecuador's southern jungle in 1956. I felt a great stirring in my heart for Ecuador after reading their most amazing story. Soon, I received a second confirmation to serve in Ecuador.

Syracuse Teen Challenge Director, David Pilch, hosted an Assembly of God Central Section Pastors' Breakfast at the Center in June of 1986. A ten-minute video documenting *The Quito Task Force* tent campaigns was shown that morning. Assembly of God Regional Director, Loren Triplett, and others presented the multiple-tent campaign project all across the capital city of Quito, Ecuador. The idea was to evangelize the capital city of Quito with eight simultaneous tent campaigns.

I was again stirred to the depths of my heart concerning serving in Ecuador. As it turned out in the years to come, Debbie and I were involved in several tent campaigns to establish churches. The campaigns were in addition to our work of church planting and education in the southern jungles of Ecuador with the Shuar Indians.

We received quite a "roasting" at our Foreign Missions Executive Committee meeting. Executive Foreign Missions Director, Philip Hogan, was exasperated with me as a candidate for foreign missions. I didn't follow the routine path. I had not senior-pastored the required two years. The two-year senior pastor requirement is usually standard protocol before one would even apply. I did have stellar references and a 97% average on my Missionary Bible Content Exam. I also had a strong recommendation from our New York District foreign Missions Director, Reverend Leon Miles. I served a total of eight years in the Syracuse Teen Challenge and Syracuse Rescue Mission. However, the lack of a single credential could be what stopped us in our tracks concerning our call to Ecuador.

During the long months of the Foreign Mission application process, I felt the Holy Spirit speak to me from Proverbs 21:1. *The King's heart is in the hand of the Lord, Like the rivers of water; He turns it wherever He wishes.* Armed with this word from the Lord, Debbie and I went ahead with the whole application process despite the doubts and fears of being rejected in the final Foreign Missions Committee (FMC) interview meeting.

When the Foreign Missions Committee met with us, they asked us to leave the room so they could have a discussion and vote on our candidacy. When the FMC finally asked us to come back into the room, we anxiously awaited the verdict that would determine our future lives and the mission's call and timing. We were on pins and needles.

Brother Hogan then stated something to this effect, "Against our better judgment, we've decided to bank on you."

Due to the intensity and negativity in his tone, I didn't realize we *were* accepted. I thought he was saying we were being turned down just by the tone of his voice. Then they all stood up and gathered around us to pray and congratulate us on our acceptance as newly appointed missionaries. (The term used today is Assemblies of God World Missionaries)

When we met Brother Hogan later in the parking lot, Debbie was still fuming at him for being so rude to me in the committee meeting.

I said, "He's only doing his job and meant nothing against us personally." I was just *so* happy we were approved!

More than thirty-five years ago, God spoke clearly and powerfully to my heart. This was *His call* on my life and not my own imagination, thoughts or desires. This would be vital to Debbie and me as we served in the mission field. We faced many difficult and heart-breaking trials in the years to come. Yet, the call remained firm and in place in our hearts. We would never give it up.

Chapter 1

Rip Tide

———◈◈———

Without a doubt, one of the most spectacular rescues of a divine nature happened in Costa Rica, April 24, 1988. We were on our way to Ecuador to begin our missionary calling after itinerating stateside for a year to raise our needed support. However, first we needed to complete a full year of language study in Costa Rica.

Debbie, our three children, Alesha, Derek, Philip, and I arrived in San Jose, Costa Rica in December of 1987 to begin a yearlong intensive, language study at the Spanish Language Institute. The Institute is located in San Francisco of the Two Rivers, a large barrio in the capital city of San Jose. The institute served fifty Christian denominations for more than sixty years. After four months of stressful classes and demanding homework, approximately twenty missionaries and their families decided to take a weekend break at the well-known Manuel Antonio Beach. It's located on the Pacific Ocean side of Costa Rica.

Before the trip, I experienced a deep unsettled feeling in the core of my gut. Perhaps it was a foreboding of something that would go wrong that weekend. In my sixty years of life

I've only had two such feelings. Both proved to be on target. It was as though the Holy Spirit was alerting me of the potential danger about to happen.

We waited more than three hours for our plane to be fixed. It became obvious that it wasn't going to happen. When we realized we wouldn't be flying that day, we decided to charter a bus instead. We boarded a very old but reliable bus for the five-hour journey in the tropical heat. Our three small children were tired and cranky when we finally arrived at midnight in Manual Antonio. What kind of a start was this for our wonderful time of relaxing and forgetting the Spanish language for a few days?

When we arrived at our hotel on the Manuel Antonio Beach, I felt hot and tired after enduring the long bus ride with three small children. The next morning, however, Debbie and I awoke to a pleasant surprise. A breakfast of fresh melon, bananas, and pineapple awaited us in the hotel's restaurant. I thought, *This is so wonderful. Perhaps it will be a great weekend after all.*

All forty of us went down to the beach. We allowed our weary brains to rest and recover from our intense studies. We relaxed as we splashed and played in the warm Pacific's aqua-blue waters. The first few hours everything was perfect. I couldn't have asked for a more ideal place to bring the children. We body surfed the waves into shore and enjoyed the warm sunshine.

After body surfing in the waist-deep water for several hours with the other families, I was tired. I headed to the beach to rest with Debbie. All of a sudden, missionary Dave Schurman, his son Jeff and his friend were swept out in a rip tide. They were about 150 feet behind us in a matter of seconds. It happened so fast it was difficult to comprehend. How had they traveled so far, so fast? The others on shore noticed at the same time I did. They began to form a human chain to try and reach them. They held hands in a vain attempt to reach the stranded missionary.

Dave held onto his eleven-year-old son with one hand and his son's friend with the other. In this predicament he was helpless to do anything except hold onto the two young boys and let the current take them where it would.

Missionary Jim Beebe and I made a quick decision to swim out to Dave and the two boys. We quickly became aware of how large and violent the waves had become. I looked back at the human chain the other missionaries were forming on the beach in an effort to reach the stranded father and two boys. It was falling apart after extending only 30-40 feet into the ocean due to the large, crashing waves. Jim and I reached the hapless trio within about a minute. Others tried to swim and help but were unable to reach us due to the violent and tumultuous seas.

When Jim and I arrived where Dave and the two boys were, I shouted over the noise of the waves, "Let go of the boys. We'll each take one and push them ahead of us toward the shore."

The struggle was intense. We swam against the riptide toward the distant shore, now 150 yards away. The large breaker waves behind us added to the extreme stress of the situation.

I fully expected to be able to swim to shore with Dave's son, Jeff. I was in the best shape of my life. I ran every day to de-stress from language study. I was even close to my personal best time of 2:02 minutes for the 800-meter track event I ran in high school. I had been a strong swimmer since childhood. My two brothers and I religiously took swim lessons after a near drowning when I was four.

I can't be sure of the time, but I estimate that four or five minutes passed as Jim, Dave, the two boys and I struggled to break free from the rip current. My confidence waned as we found ourselves further away from shore than when we started. Due to the intense struggle, the lactic acid built up in my shoulders and arms. It became so severe that I couldn't even lift my arms out of the water to take a stroke. I started to sink.

With my pride and self-sufficiency now stripped from me, I felt the strong and eminent sentence of death. Not only couldn't I save this 11-year-old boy, but I couldn't even save myself from drowning in those violent waves.

In stark desperation, I cried out, "JESUS, SAVE US!"

I hadn't cried out earlier because I didn't want to frighten the boys. Now, since we were going to die anyway, what difference did it make if they were scared.

All of a sudden, a very large wave literally picked all five of us up and sent us plummeting toward the shore against the outgoing riptide. Immediately, a second wave came up behind us, as if on cue, to continue the spectacular ride. Then as on cue, a third wave finished our journey toward the shore and deposited us in shallow waters. We completed our journey by walking the last twenty feet to dry land. Without any strength left, we fell down on the beach and praised God for this dramatic and divine rescue from certain death. We found out later that there had been numerous deaths by drowning due to the rip tides on that particular beach over the years. As I write this chapter and remember that fateful day many years ago, I can still feel myself riding those three huge rolling waves out of danger and marveling at God's power to deliver. Amen!

The lesson I learned is that God didn't send the rescuing waves *until* we cried out for help, like Peter when he was sinking beneath the waves (Matthew 14:28-31). When we come to the end of our strength, God will step in *if* we ask Him.

*They see the works of the Lord, And His wonders in the deep. For He commands and raises the stormy wind, which lifts up the waves of the sea. They mount up to the heavens, they go down again to the depths: Their soul melts because of trouble. They reel to and fro, and stagger like a drunken man, **and*** *are at their wits' end. Then they cry out to the Lord in their trouble, And He brings them out of their distresses. He calms the storm, so that its waves are still. Then they are glad because they are quiet; so **He guides them to their desired haven.** Oh, that men would give thanks to the Lord for His goodness, And for His wonderful works to the children of men!* (Psalm 107:24-31, emphasis added).

* * * *

Update: Dave Sherman's son, Jeff, whom I attempted to save from the rip tides, returned to Ecuador after his graduation from college in the States 24 years later. He became a high school teacher. My youngest daughter, Abby, was one of his students. He was also Abby's biggest financial supporter for her mission's trip to Africa in 2012.

Chapter 2

Miraculous Stunt Driving

———————⟨◇⟩⟨◇⟩———————

My second and equally dramatic great escape from death came when I returned from the jungle on September 21, 2007. I ministered in the jungle village of Kusutka in the Morona Santiago Province for a week of Bible teaching and leadership meetings before the incident occurred. My custom for the previous twenty years was to drive from Quito to Shell (a 4- or 5-hour drive) and park the car. Then I flew in by Cessna airplane with Christian pilot, Rick LaBoeff, or Mission Aviation Fellowship. We landed on the dirt runway of Kusutka forty miles in deep jungle, southeast of Shell. There was no road access. From my main base village of Kusutka, I regularly hiked the muddy paths for hours, but I was always accompanied by Shuar men to evangelize and disciple the surrounding villages.

Scheduling didn't allow me to be picked up for the return 22-minute flight from Kusutka to Shell until late afternoon. We landed on the airstrip in Shell at 5:00 p.m. This meant I had to drive back to Quito most of the way in the dark. I typically tried to avoid driving at night but many times couldn't.

I was very grateful to the Assemblies of God youth department for providing us with new and reliable cars for our transportation needs as foreign missionaries. Our 2003 Mitsubishi Montero was no exception. With high ground clearance and seating for seven people (we had five children), it also had a great reputation for mechanical reliability. As far as I was concerned, the only drawback was that it was unstable turning at higher speeds due to being somewhat top heavy because of its narrow wheel base.

By the time I loaded my gear and filled up with gas for the trip home, it was 5:30 p.m. I would have an hour of light and the remaining three or four hours would be in the dark. All went well the first two hours. I made good time until traffic picked up as I neared the city of Latacunga at 7:30 p.m. I was traveling on The Pan American Highway, the principle transportation artery that runs north and south connecting most Ecuadorian cities. Most of the highway was two lanes. However, on large hills and entrances to cities it changed into four lanes to accommodate the greater amount of traffic.

As I traveled downhill on a four-lane section of the highway, I noticed a car parked in the extreme right lane with his lights on. It was about sixty yards ahead of me when all of a sudden it began a left-hand turn across traffic directly in front of me!

Due to the shock and adrenaline that pumped into my mind, everything seemed to shift into slow motion. The over-powering thought that instantly hit me was, *there is no way for you to get out of this accident; it will be fatal.* There were several cars slightly behind me on my right and five or six cars coming from the opposite direction toward me. No barrier separated my lanes from the oncoming traffic. In this scenario I was "designated" to be the one to hit the car crossing the highway. I was pinned on my right side by cars and on the left with lanes of oncoming traffic. I thought, *I'm done for, I can't get out of this.*

However, with the thought of ensuing death came a cry for help from the depth of my being.

Without enough time to even uselessly honk my horn, I cried out, "Jesus!"

Simultaneously, I yanked the steering wheel hard left. I yanked it so violently in a last-ditch effort to avoid the car directly in front of me that I rocked my SUV up onto its left two wheels. I was driving nearly sixty miles per hour on two wheels and about to crash into the car crossing the four-lane highway. After the initial impact, we would both be hit multiple times by the traffic coming from both directions. In those fractions of a second, this was what I was preparing for and totally expecting to happen.

I winced my eyes, tightened my grip on the steering wheel, and got ready for the fatal impact. I MISSED! I can't explain how, but I passed by the car crossing the highway without hitting it.

Now, I faced a new problem. I missed the crossing car but left my side of the highway in the process. I found myself in the lanes of on-coming traffic, still driving on my left two wheels. Whoosh, whoosh, whoosh. I missed the first car, then the second, then the third. I wove in and out of the on-coming traffic like a well-choreographed Hollywood chase scene with professional stunt drivers. It was the most terrifying and exhilarating experience of my life as I prepared to die every second for eight seconds. It seemed to last forever. When the traffic finally cleared on both sides of the highway, I was able to drive over to my side. I set down the Montero with a loud thump back onto all four wheels, untouched by other cars. I was so traumatized by the incident I drove thirty miles per hour all the way back to Quito. I needed the time to recuperate.

Conclusion

There are five things I know for sure:

1. I know I don't possess the skills or ability to drive like that, period.

2. I know God sent angels to steady and steer the car to prevent me from rolling over and colliding with other cars on the highway.

3. I know that if I hadn't cried out, "Jesus," I wouldn't be alive today. God answers prayer. Time and distance don't limit Him in any way.

4. I know how important it is to always keep your heart in a state where you are able to cry out to Jesus anytime day or night.

5. I know He is always ready and able to help.

Yes, we had the sentence of death in ourselves, that we should not trust in ourselves but in God who raises the dead, who delivered us from so great a death, and does deliver us; in whom we trust that He will still deliver us (2 Corinthians 1:9-10).

This poor man cried out, and the Lord heard him. And saved him... The angel of the Lord encamps all around those who fear Him, and delivers them (Psalm 34:6-7).

Chapter 3

A 400-Foot Cliff

✦✦✦

Many times from 1990 to 2015, I walked from the Shuar village of Kusutka in the Morona Santiago Province, to the village of Kuakash in the Pastaza Province of Ecuador. Traveling from one province to another involved crossing a very fast-moving and dangerous river called the Pastaza. It's a major tributary of the great Amazon River of South America. Crossing it is always an adventure. At its narrowest point it's 250 yards across, with multiple other branches that also need to be crossed. Many of the branches require wading through waist or chest-deep water for more than a mile.

One of the really exciting parts of the river crossing is getting down *to* the river. I usually choose a 400-foot, wall-like path that becomes very slippery and dangerous after it rains, and it rains *all* the time. If it's too dangerous, I'll use the path that's a mile longer but goes down to the river more gradually through the jungle.

Once, in a 30-foot, carved-out canoe, my job was simply to not tip over the unstable canoe while two young, strong Shuar Indians paddled their hearts out to cross to the other side.

Sometimes the river current is so strong and treacherous that we must wait many hours, sometimes days, to safely cross over.

In the spring of 1995, I hiked between the villages of Kumai and Kuakash with Shuar Pastor Rueben. At that time, the path ran along the edge of the 400-foot precipice. There were several places during the two-hour hike where the path literally took us right up to the very edge. We had to be extremely careful or we'd slip and fall to our death. It almost happened to me.

As I walked thirty feet in front of Rueben, on the edge of the cliff, I suddenly lost my orientation and stumbled inches from the great drop. Instantly, Rueben was at my side and grabbed my arm to keep me from falling down that 400-foot wall. He was there just in the nick of time. A fraction of a second later and I would have fallen.

I was stunned. Why did I suddenly become disoriented and lose balance at the most dangerous part of the path? I walked this path many times prior with no such problems, and I don't have a fear of heights. Also, I can't explain or understand how Rueben could have possibly moved quick enough to grab me and keep me from falling. He was at least thirty feet behind me when I stumbled. Two Bible verses came to mind in this particular situation. *Be sober, be vigilant; because your adversary the devil walks about like a roaring lion, seeking whom he may devour* (1 Peter 5:8). And, *For He shall give His angels charge over you, to keep you in all your ways. In their hands they shall bear you up, lest you dash your foot against a stone* (Psalm 91:11-12). The lesson I learned in that near tragedy was to never forget the invisible, yet real, spiritual warfare we must live in and pass through while on the earth. Also, God is able to protect us and keep us safe until we enter His heavenly kingdom.

I believe God allows such experiences as wake up calls and warnings to *not* let our guard down. He uses them as reminders for us to continually look to Him for our protection and the protection of others though our prayers.

> *Now to Him who is able to keep you from stumbling, and to present you faultless before the presence of His glory with exceeding joy, to God our Savior, who alone is wise, be glory and majesty, dominion and power, both now and forever. Amen* (Jude 24:25).

Chapter 4

The Hitchhiker

———————◇✕◇———————

I t was mid-February 1989. We arrived in Quito from language school in Costa Rica at the end of December and had only been in Ecuador a little over six weeks. I felt deep in my heart that part of our calling to Ecuador involved working with indigenous tribes in the jungle. We had been in contact with our area director, Paul Hutsell, as well as Mission Aviation Fellowship pilot, Jim Manley.

Debbie and I decided to participate in the Ecuadoran holiday, Carnival, and travel down to Shell-Mera, Puyo and Tena. Our intention was to explore ministry possibilities and get to know Ecuador better. We loaded the three children, Alesha (5), Derek (3½), and Philip (2), into our 1981 Chevy Blazer.

We drove south through Quito then traveled through the cities of Latacunga, Ambato and Banos on our way to Puyo. As we rounded the corner on the Banos-Puyo pass, we left the mountains and dropped in elevation rapidly to the jungle. I was in awe of the beauty and expanse of the Pastaza River and the jungle. We crossed over into a completely different world with exotic animals, big bugs, and wildlife that I had never seen except in magazines and on television.

The next several days, we talked to local folks and explored the towns of Shell and Puyo. Sunday, we started up the Puyo-Tena-Quito road which was all dirt. We knew it would be a longer trip back to Quito, but we wanted to see the towns of Tena, Baeza, and Papallacta. Debbie noticed Alesha felt warm before we arrived in Tena about 2:00 in the afternoon. She gave her some baby aspirin and put a damp cloth on her head to keep her cool. About an hour later, Alesha was burning hot with a fever. We couldn't get it down even with the air conditioning in the car on high.

She was on Debbie's lap when all of a sudden her eyes rolled back in her head and she lost consciousness. She went into a grand-mal seizure. Now we were really scared. We prayed and cried out to God. Derek and Philip, being so little, reacted to our panic. They were crying in the back seat. After a desperate hour of driving in search of a hospital, we entered the small town of Baeza. We asked if there was a clinic or hospital nearby. The hospital and town clinic were both closed due to the holiday. One helpful woman put perfume on Alesha and told us it would cool her down. Nothing we did with the wet cloth or the perfume did anything to bring her out of the seizure. It had already been more than an hour. We knew we were at least several hours away from Quito and now feared irreparable brain damage in our precious little five-year-old daughter. No one could help us. We continued to pray and ask the Lord for help. We felt so helpless, frustrated, and fearful. To make matters worse, we were low on gas. We had less than 1/8 of a tank. I hadn't seen a gas station since Tena. This compounded an already desperate situation.

I spotted a gas station a few miles outside of Baeza and pulled in. Unfortunately, even the gas stations were shut down on Carnival. All the pumps were locked up and no one was there. I drove away frustrated. I didn't know what to do next. I pulled over to the side of the road.

I put my head down on the steering wheel and prayed, "Oh Lord Jesus, we really need your help NOW! Our daughter is dying, we're almost out of gas, and we're far from home. Please help us. Direct our steps. We still trust in you."

When I lifted my head, I saw an eighty-year-old man hitch-hiking right in front of me. I turned to Debbie and said, "I feel like we should pick him up."

It wasn't that unusual for me. I picked up hitchhikers state-side for years to witness to them about Christ. But this was different. I felt *he* could help *us*.

"Get in," I said to him in Spanish. "Do you know where there is a gas station nearby?"

He motioned for me to return to the gas station I just left. He insisted that I return. So I did.

"Honk the horn," he instructed me.

I did.

After several minutes, a yawning young man came out of a small windowless building, unlocked the pumps, and filled my gas tank. I was amazed. Evidently, business was slow and he was probably sleeping off his late night celebration of Carnival from the night before.

Then I asked the old man if there was a hospital nearby to help our daughter.

He said, "Yes, just turn around and go back to where you just came from."

"You mean away from Quito?" I replied.

"Yes," he said.

Now I was in a quandary. I didn't want to drive *away* from what I perceived as my only hope to help my daughter. She had now been unconscious for more than 75 minutes.

I paused and prayed again, "Lord, please let me know if this is from You."

I felt it was. But as a father, it wasn't an easy decision.

We drove very quickly back down the highway in the direction we just came from. After several miles, the road forked eastward in the direction of the northern jungle town of Lago Agrio. Now I was really worried. Where was he taking us?

The old man seemed confident of where we were going, and was now comforting Derek and Philip in the back seat. Debbie drove as I held Alesha in my arms and prayed for a miracle. This was the first time Debbie attempted to drive in Ecuador. To make matters even worse, she now had uncontrollable diarrhea due to intense stress.

Soon we arrived in the small town of Chaco. The old man directed us to an old dirt road that led us into a field. Now I thought he was really crazy and leading us on a wild goose chase. I started to think that I shouldn't have listed to him or allowed a stranger to put my daughter's life in jeopardy. We drove past cows and pigs. This was a desolate area.

I was about to tell Debbie to turn around when a huge hospital building came into view. As we pulled up to the building, we were instructed to go around to the other side and ring the bell next to the door. We did. All of a sudden, several Catholic nuns came rushing out to meet us. They took us into the emergency room and injected Alesha with medicine to bring her out of the 90-minute seizure. Within minutes, she was conscience and started to cool down from her burning fever. They even gave Debbie meds to stop her diarrhea.

We were so, so thankful to God, to this old man and to the Catholic Hospital out in the middle of nowhere. We thanked the nuns profusely and were soon on our way back to Quito.

The old man continued to comfort our two boys like a loving grandpa and visited with us as we drove. He even directed our route when we would have gotten lost. We entered the town of Pifo, and he indicated that he needed to be let out. Quito was right in front of us and we couldn't get lost. As he smiled and waved to us, the thought came to me, *was he an angel sent by God to help us?* Human or angelic, he was definitely sent from God.

Chapter 5

The Jaguar Visit

⟫⟪

It was the summer of 1996. Dr. Ron Lamb and Rick Salvado, P.A. (working through Healthcare Ministries of AGWM) joined me to minister in the southern jungles of Ecuador. We worked in my two hub villages of Kusutka and Kumay. Kusutka is located in the Morona Santiago province. Whereas, Kumay is located in the Pastaza province near the Pastaza River.

Our trip down to the jungle from Quito was quite normal and uneventful until we entered the Baños-Puyo pass. At that time, there was a narrow single-lane passage for the first seven or eight miles as you traveled toward the towns of Rio Verde and Rio Negro. Both of these jungle towns were located pre cariously close to the great precipice that dropped hundreds of feet to the Pastaza River.

A rather impressive waterfall fell right on this old rural highway just past the first tunnel on the outskirts of Baños. I usually used the waterfall as my own personal carwash when I traveled to the jungle. When Ron, Rick, and I neared the hidden waterfall, I stopped the car and encouraged them to get on top of the truck luggage rack. It had reinforced steel that could easily support the two men. I told them to enjoy the spectacular view coming up soon. Later, I'd send up their cameras so they could take advantage of the tropical scenery we would be passing. They got up there on the roof thinking they were kings of the world. Then I turned the corner and drove straight through the waterfall. They got drenched. They screamed, yelled, and laughed the entire three seconds it took us to pass through it. Then I mercifully handed up their cameras.

I told them, "It's not a good idea to bring cameras into the shower."

The time spent in the jungle over the next week was packed with ministry and work. Rick and Ron saw patients from early morning to late at night. They told me that they would love to return to the jungle another time to spend a week hiking from village to village.

I said, "You have an open invitation anytime you can get free."

I'm still waiting, but I'm sure they'll be back someday.

Ron, Rick, and I had a very long day with the medical and dental clinic. At the end of the day, Ron checked the teeth of Pastor Ernesto's father. He was over eighty years old and had prayed forty years for missionaries to come to his village of Kuakash with the Gospel of Christ.

He walked the three hour hike up to the village of Kumay to have his teeth examined. As Dr. Ron checked his teeth, he gently lifted out one of his large molars from the lower back of his jaw. It simply came out when Dr. Ron pulled on it with his fingers. Talk about having a loose tooth. Ernesto's father was so grateful for the relief that came from having that rotten tooth out of his mouth. I saw him from time to time over the years walking with his wife many hours away from his village well into his eighties. He died about ten years ago and is now with the Lord.

The last night we were in Kumay, we camped under mosquito

nets in a small hut with no door. We had been eating the meat of a recently butchered cow for three days. The villagers hung the meat close to our hut and ten feet off the ground. Evidently, animals in the jungle could also smell the meat hanging in the tree because we had a visitor that night.

The jungle can be a very noisy place to sleep if it's not raining. My custom is to always use earplugs, because I'm a very light sleeper.

When Ron, Rick, and I woke up the next morning, Ron said, "Did you hear the loud, deep growl last night?"

I replied, "No, my ears were plugged. I didn't hear a thing."

Rick added, "The little jungle dogs barked like crazy for about a half an hour. Then came that loud growl like a lion. Then it got quiet again and stayed quiet the rest of the night."

When I got out of my mosquito net and crossed the three feet to the open entrance of our jungle hut, I spotted a paw print as large as my hand.

Ron said to me, "That's a jaguar print no more than a few feet from where your head was laying, Tim."

I gasped in amazement and great relief. I slept through a confrontation with a big jungle cat and a bunch of barking dogs guarding the meat hanging in the tree over our hut. I thank God for His protection when we didn't even know we needed it. I wonder how many times that has happened in our lives.

He shall cover you with his feathers, and under His wings you shall take refuge; His truth shall be your shield and buckler. You shall not be afraid of the terror by night (Psalm 91:4-5).

Chapter 6

A Prisoner Called Enrique

———— ⟡⟡ ————

Debbie and I arrived in Quito, Ecuador, late in December of 1988. Debbie, Alesha, and I came down with hepatitis A after being in country only six weeks. This really knocked us for a loop physically. This disease usually does. With three small children to care for, it made it very difficult to rest and recover. There was no way I could enter the jungle that first year as I struggled to regain my own health.

After five months or so, my strength began to come back. Along with my strength came a great desire to minister God's word. I found out where the two main prisons were located and went by myself to see what I could do. The men's prison, Garcia Moreno, had many different areas where the prisoners were housed. I literally wandered into a place called the CDP. It was a kind of holding area for the men until they were sentenced. Sentencing sometimes took two or three years to happen.

The open courtyard of the CDP held around 150-200 men. They usually walked for exercise and talked with other prisoners or visitors. Wednesday was a visiting day. It was also the reason I was able to get in without a special pass. I spotted a group of about thirty men and began to preach the salvation message of Christ from my Spanish Bible. They were shocked at my boldness to just start a meeting in the middle of their courtyard unannounced and uninvited. Through the conviction of the Holy Spirit I felt that He was getting through to these men. After about ten minutes of preaching, I had completely exhausted my very limited Spanish vocabulary. Then I had an alter call for any who wanted to come forward and receive Christ as Savior. To my utter amazement, about ten men came forward. I had them kneel with me right there on the dirty cement floor and repeat the sinner's prayer. After we all rose to our feet, I continued to exhort them about living the Christ centered life. I emphasized the importance of reading and studying God's word.

My joy and excitement was great in those moments immediately following the salvation prayer with the ten prisoners but it was short lived. As soon as I dismissed my newly-saved Christian prisoners, I thought to myself, *I have to come back soon and continue teaching these new believers.* As instructed by the prisoners nearby, I clanked the lock and chain against the metal door to indicate to the prison guard to come let me out. He was down the hall and out of sight forty feet away. I soon discovered that he would only come when he was good and ready and it wouldn't be anytime soon. I was ready to leave the prison courtyard and couldn't due to a lazy and unresponsive guard.

I turned around to face the courtyard again. This time I noticed the walls around me and the prisoners milling around. Then I realized something very disturbing. There wasn't a single guard in the whole prison courtyard. Furthermore, I was the only white face in the prison. I started to become really nervous when a gang of twelve men approached me. Their intent didn't look friendly. They surrounded me and knew I was out of my element. I was alone and there were no guards to protect me.

They began to talk harshly and go through my pockets to steal my wallet. They couldn't find anything. I wore a security wallet that attaches to my belt and tucks under my pants hidden from sight. Thank God.

When they couldn't find a wallet to steal, I regained my composure somewhat and told them to back off. After several minutes, they did. Finally, the guard behind the wall came. He unlocked the door and let me out. He was completely oblivious to what just happened, but I was traumatized by my close encounter with the prisoners. It was as though I heard a voice in my mind say, *If this is how they treat you on your first visit, how much worse will it be later on? Don't go back to the prison or it will be worse for you. Do not go back.*

I really struggled the next several days with that decision. As I prayed to determine if I should go back or not, I felt the calm inner-assurance of the Holy Spirit saying I was supposed to go back. After all, look at the hunger and humility for God's word. Those ten men who knelt with me to receive Christ made it worth the danger and risk to go back in and keep preaching. So I went with fear and trembling. Back I went into that dark, evil, and claustrophobic courtyard. Again, I preached to a group of men milling around. This time, only one man came forward to receive Christ. His name was Enrique. He was a large, powerfully-built Ecuadorian black man. He knelt with me to pray. Afterward, he rose to his feet with me to a new life in Christ.

I was puzzled by the poor response to my altar call. *Only one. Well, that's God's business. My business is to preach His Word. His business is to touch hearts.* I continued to visit the prison courtyard to preach. I was usually there three times per week. Sometimes I preached three and four times per day in the different areas of this large maximum-security men's prison. I soon noticed that Enrique always positioned himself in front of me while I preached in the courtyard. He stood just off to my left side in military fashion with his head and eyes staring straight forward. His feet were spread about twelve inches apart angled outward with his arms locked behind his back. He stood alert yet comfortable. My Marine Corp. Officer Training made me acutely aware of these physical cues. Evidently, Enrique had some military training. I didn't understand Enrique's reason for positioning himself this way until a few weeks later.

Like the first time I experienced a near assault from a gang of prisoners, it happened again. I had just finished the altar call, when another group of prisoners began to approach me. This time it was different. Boy, was it different. Enrique, who was positioned right in front of me, came alive and looked directly at the leader of this new group of prisoners. He raised and lowered his head ever so slightly. The reaction from the leader and the group was immediate and apparent. They quickly backed away from me and never returned.

I learned three things about Enrique that day which I hadn't known before. First, that he knew how to communicate without words. Second, that he was the most powerful and feared prisoner in the whole population of Garcia Moreno Prison. And third, when he signals with his eyes to back away from the preacher, you better do it quickly and quietly. Never again in my many years of preaching in the prison did I ever have any trouble with gangs or individual prisoners trying to rob or harass me. Thank God for men like Enrique, who use their gift of helps for the glory of God and the protection of His servants.

Michael, one of the chief princes, came to help me,
for I had been left alone there with the kings of
Persia (Daniel 10:13).

Enrique, like the archangel Michael, was sent to help me.

Chapter 7

Six-Month Battle in Prayer

One of the things God used to direct Debbie and me to Ecuador was a video clip shown in the Syracuse Teen Challenge Center about the Quito Task Force in Ecuador. The Quito Task Force coordinated and administrated multiple, large evangelistic tent campaigns simultaneously throughout the city of Quito, Ecuador, from 1986 to 1992. With this in mind, we brought a large 500-person tent. We used our shipping container to transport the tent to Ecuador in 1988.

After the better part of a year in Ecuador, Debbie, Alesha, and I recovered from our severe case of hepatitis A. We formed close relationships with, Arturo Espinel and Galo Benitez, two Ecuadorian pastors interested in having a tent campaign.

We located a community with absolutely no evangelical church and a quickly growing population. We rented a half-acre lot for thirty dollars per month with a two-year contract. Our evangelist was a former atheist and communist professor. His name was Dr. Luis Flores. He experienced a radical transformation to Christ due to the prayer and fasting of his wife and daughter during a Gigi Avila evangelistic campaign here in Quito in 1985.

Our tent campaign schedule was seven nights a week for the first two years. This was in addition to our other outreach ministries and leadership meetings. We built a solid congregation of 300 people by the second year. Now I began to worry about where we would go when our rent contract was up in six months. To make things worse, we had to leave soon for our one-year furlough. We had already spent a year in language school and three years in Ecuador.

The landlord of the property adamantly refused to talk about extending the rent contract or selling us the property. In fact, he actively pursued ways to get us off the property after only one year. We looked around the barrio and found no alternatives. After much prayer, we felt God wanted us to stay where we were and pray for a miracle, but it would be a battle.

We decided to pray at the tent site Monday through Friday mornings, for two hours, until an answer came. So we prayed in desperation with no Plan B. Sometimes there was eight to ten people and other times only two or three. Many mornings I was there all alone with God. But there was *always*, without fail, someone praying every cold, damp morning on that mountain in San Isidro del Inca in North Quito. It seemed like nothing was happening. Yet, mighty things were happening in the invisible world. The six-month timeframe was coming to a close. There were just a few more days until Debbie and I left for furlough.

Pastor Arturo got a call out of the blue from the very stubborn land owner. He agreed to sell the property. We were literally down to the wire. God revealed his plan and purpose through His church when we didn't give up on prayer. The faith of the new congregation grew by leaps and bounds when they saw first-hand, direct answer to prayer in a situation that seemed impossible. Even today, there remains a thriving congregation that has been light and salt in that community for more than twenty-seven years.

The landlord ended up selling us the property, approximately 1,500 square yards, for $23,000 USD in 1992. Today it's valued at more than $500,000 USD. The whole region has greatly developed in the last twenty-seven years. It's also interesting that, because of our ceaseless prayer, he sold us the property against his own will. After finalizing the sale, he was angry with himself, but it was too late. We had the deed in our hands with every legal requirement completed. In a small way, I liken this particular landlord to Pharaoh who did not want to free the children of Israel. Pharaoh even said, *Why have we done this?* (Exodus 14:5). He tried to pursue them and bring them back as slaves to the Egyptians but couldn't because God was on their side. He delivered them and protected them.

> *Praying always with all prayer and supplication in the spirit, being watchful to this end; **and having done all to stand**!* (Ephesians 6:18, 13, emphasis added).

Chapter 8

You Will Tread on Serpents

———————— ⟡⟡ ————————

It was May of 1999. The trip to the jungle had been set up nearly a year in advance. I warned the twenty young men and women from the Rockford, Illinois, Assembly of God Church, that they needed to be in really good physical shape to hike the four hours between Campamento Ayuy and Kusutka. The two villages in the Southern jungle of Ecuador, where they would be ministering with me.

With so many students, tents, food and supplies, we needed to make seven flights into the jungle using Missionary Aviation Fellowship to get us there from Macas, Ecuador. It took the whole day, but we all made it in. To God be the praise.

Campamento Ayuy was our first village. At least fifteen people gave their lives to Christ during the three-day ministry period. We baptized the newly-saved converts in the Pastaza River. The river was so swift and strong that we had to hold onto them so the river wouldn't carry them away. The church services at night were powerful. The Masters Commission students ministered in song, drama, and testimony. During the day, the mission team focused on children and teen programs.

They kept the whole village engaged as God's Word and His Spirit found a way deep into their hungry hearts.

When the fourth day arrived, we hiked to Kusutka village to minister there as well. My great concern with such a large group hiking the knee-deep muddy paths was the poisonous bush master snakes (aka: x-snakes). They kill approximately five percent of the Shuar population with their venom. During a torrential downpour, we prayed for Jesus' divine protection against the dreaded x-snakes as well as strength to be able to get safely to the next village.

We started the hike together. Our group consisted of Pastor Onelio Gonzalez, myself, twenty Masters Commission team members and approximately twelve Shuar Indians who helped us carry the tents and equipment.

After an hour of hiking, several Shuar men came up behind me talking in excited voices.

They said, "Brother Tim, the leader of the young men has fainted and is passed out in the mud a half mile behind you. Come quickly and help him!"

Immediately, I walked back to the leader who was laying down and barely conscience. I got him to sit up and gave him some water and some cookies I carried in my backpack. He recovered quickly and got to his feet. He had helped everyone else prepare for the hike and failed to eat or drink anything himself. Thus, he fainted an hour into the hike. I asked one of the Shuar Indians to carry his eighty-pound backpack. He and I continued our hike together toward Kusutka village in a slow but steady manner.

By now, the rest of the mission team was ahead of us by twenty minutes. After hiking several miles, we climbed a fairly steep, muddy hill. When we reached the summit, I noticed something unusual in the middle of the path. It was a snake out in the open and prepared to strike. I had never seen anything quite like it before, and I had seen many snakes as I grew up in rural Upstate New York and many in my years of hiking through the jungles of Ecuador. Snakes stay low and try to hide when someone walks near them. This snake wanted to strike even though we were still more than one hundred feet away. When we got close enough, I identified it as the dreaded and deadly x-snake of Ecuador. When we were within fifteen feet of it, we observed that it was muddy, and that it was angry.

It dawned on me what must have happened. Several minutes earlier, the missions group from the States unknowingly trampled one of the deadliest snakes in the world without anyone getting bit. The realization of God's divine protection hit me like a bolt of lightning. We praised the Lord for His abundant mercy and power. We praised Him for the answer to our prayer for protection that we prayed earlier in the rain. Then I picked up a stick near me, struck the snake, and killed it.

It didn't dawn on me until years later that God made the snake stay there in that striking position until we arrived. He showed that He is a prayer-answering God who delights to help and protect us when we pray. By causing the snake to stay in striking position, we would know that He heard and answered our prayer for protection.

Many tears were shed by the mission team as well as the Shuar children when it was time for us to leave the jungle.

You shall tread upon the lion and the cobra. The young lion and the serpent you shall trample underfoot (Psalm 91:13).

Chapter 9

Spiritual Warfare at Teen Challenge

This story took place at Syracuse Teen Challenge in the early 1980's. Although it didn't happen on the mission field, it served as a powerful training experience to prepare me.

Tony, a thirty-year-old man with major drug addictions and many other problems, came to the center from Canada. He received Christ as Savior ten years earlier but it didn't stick. We soon found out why.

Tony's grandmother was a high-category practicing witch, involved in the deep darkness of occult practices. She had a satanic covenant placed on Tony when he was only four years old. Since that time, he had extraordinary spiritual powers at his command. He possessed the power of astral projection, which allowed his spirit to travel to other locations. He was able to make people obey him and had power over physical demonic visitations wherever he was. His satanic powers were strong because Satan's control over him was strong.

As a thirty-year-old man, he tried desperately to break free from a life-long enslavement to the enemy of our souls. This was not going to be easy. Every day from the time of Tony's arrival at Teen Challenge, he placed his own hands around his neck, went into a demonic convulsion, and tried to commit suicide. This went on day after day, week after week, and month after month, for four months. Curt Doe, Barry Pendergrass, Lee Conway and myself attempted to hold him down as he violently reacted to our intense prayers. Tony was slight and weighed about 120 pounds, but he threw us all over the place. Over the course of six major prayer sessions within that four-month period, literally thousands of unclean spirits (demons) came out of him as we commanded them. Yet, in spite of all that deliverance, Tony was still not free. He still attempted to choke himself to death every day. We were frustrated and at wits end. I had to go and ask my mentor, Harry Sharples, about this difficult case.

Harry was a ninety-year-old prayer warrior, prophet, and man of the Word. He had a deep relationship with Christ. I spent many hours with him over several years. I met him when I left my banking career to work at Teen Challenge. He had ministered alongside Evangelist Smith Wigglesworth. Wigglesworth raised twenty-seven people from the dead during his storied and extraordinary life.

I met with Harry and asked, "Why isn't Tony free after all that prayer and fasting for deliverance?"

Harry replied in his Welsh accent, "Oh Brother Timmy, don't you know that God will never deliver us from our friends, only our enemies."

He then quoted to me Psalm 139:21-22. *Do I not hate them, O Lord, who hate You? And do I not loathe those who rise up against You? I hate them with perfect hatred; I count them my enemies.*

That was the key to Tony's total and complete deliverance. He had to learn to hate, despise, and utterly reject the demonic powers who sought to keep control of him and destroy him. They had been with him throughout his whole life. They had given him power, money, and prestige. Now he was afraid of them. Not only that, he wasn't sure he believed that God could protect him from them.

When I saw Tony the next day, he was in his usual state of convulsions with his hands wrapped around his neck.

I shouted into his ear, "Tony these demonic powers are NOT your friends. They are your enemies and they are trying to kill you. Jesus is all powerful and He will protect you."

Again, and again, and again I shouted these truths into Tony's spirit for more than an hour. Finally, something clicked inside Tony's brain. He accepted this new perspective and aligned his will with God's will. The four major powers controlling Tony came out with a big whoosh. The four demons were suicide, witchcraft, sorcery, and death. We had commanded them to identify themselves prior to this. Death was the principle ruler over all the others. But it left when Tony cried out from the depths of his heart for Jesus to deliver him from his enemies.

Then he received the most powerful infilling of the Holy Spirit I have ever seen. He immediately spoke with other tongues and glorified God in the most marvelous stream of praise and worship. This lasted for more than an hour. We all worshipped God with Tony for this most extraordinary and long sought-after victory over the enemy. Tony quickly rose up in spiritual leadership within the center.

We learned many things during that four-month battle. First of all, never give up. Secondly, be alert and know your enemy. Thirdly, hate your enemy and give him no opportunity. Finally, be filled with the Holy Spirit and the power of His Word.

After this experience, I renewed my covenant with the Holy Spirit to never give Satan room in my life to control me, especially in the area of alcohol and sexual sin. I committed myself to always strive to maintain an abiding and intimate relationship with the Lord. This has kept me focused and protected on the mission field. Amen. I learned to not fear the enemy after that battle. He must always yield to Jesus' superior power. I hope this insider knowledge is beneficial to others. It cost me dearly to obtain it.

> *Finally, my brethren, be strong in the Lord and in the power of his might. Put on the whole armor of God, that you may be able to stand against the wiles of the devil. For we do not wrestle against flesh and blood, but against principalities, against powers, against the rulers of the darkness of this age, against the spiritual hosts of wickedness in the heavenly places* (Ephesians 6:10-12).

Chapter 10

Amazing Timing

———————⟡⟡⟡———————

I t was May 2007. Pastor Jorge Ailla and I visited the villages
of Timias, Tsunki, Tumbien, and were back in Kusutka to
be flown out by MAF (Mission Aviation Fellowship) Monday
morning.

As we packed to leave, Luis Chiriap came into the bunk-
house. He had received a message that the Ecuadorian Air Force
indefinitely cancelled *all* flights into the jungle. Two pilots were
already being detained in nearby villages for political reasons.
Both pilots were released after the Shuar of those villages could
ascertain the reason they landed in their villages. This whole
scenario was largely due to unauthorized oil company repre-
sentatives working with greedy Shuar Indians to scope out
possible drilling areas in the jungle. This was contrary to the
Shuar Federation's stance and policy at the time.

It was 9:00 a.m. when Luis gave us the message. Needless
to say, we were shocked. Nothing like this had ever happened
in the Ecuadorian jungle before.

Jorge and I started talking through our options. We had
been in the jungle for seven days and needed to return to Quito.

We still had responsibilities to our work and ministries there. Two young men in the village, Alejandro and Tito, heard of our dilemma and encouraged us to walk out with them to be able to catch the 6:00 p.m. bus. The bus stop was located approximately twenty-four miles from Kusutka village. Their exhortations and encouraging words soon had Jorge and I packing for the unplanned hike. Both of us hiked this path in the past and knew we had a long day ahead of us.

We left the village at 9:30 in the morning with heavy backpacks and two Shuar Indian youth as our guides. After four hours and six demanding mountain rises, we arrived at the jungle village of Macuma. We were exhausted and sat down to rest for five minutes. The longer part of the hike was still ahead of us.

All of the sudden, a twelve-passenger plane landed on Macuma's runway. Alejandro and Tito ran to check out the airplane. In less than ten minutes we were on the plane and leaving the jungle. I leaned back in the comfortable seat as we flew high above the thick jungle and thanked God for his mercy. He miraculously brought us out of the jungle. If we arrived in Macuma five minutes earlier or later we never would have been able to board that plane on time. I have no idea what that plane was even doing in the jungle when *all* flights had been suspended by the Ecuadorian National Government. It was all so amazing. I was on an airplane avoiding eight more hours of arduous hiking.

Then the reality of our situation hit me. My watch now read 1:45 p.m. If we hadn't miraculously caught the plane, we wouldn't have made it out of the jungle in time to catch the last bus at 6:00 p.m. We would have been three and a half hours late. We would have still been deep in the jungle after dark and totally unprepared for the night. We had no hut or tent to sleep in and would have been totally exposed to the elements. We were not prepared to protect ourselves against blood sucking bats, poisonous snakes, 250-pound jaguars, all kinds of tarantulas, deadly, black scorpions, and the many other wild creatures.

I can't thank Him enough for rescuing us when we didn't even realize that we needed rescuing.

He leads me in the paths of righteousness for His name's sake (Psalm 23:3).

Chapter 11

The Almost-Assault in Manta

———◇◇◇———

We had just hosted a youth evangelism team from our home church, Grace Assembly of God, and sister church, Trinity Assembly of God, both in the Syracuse, New York, area. It was July 2001. My nephew and niece, Ben and Becky, stayed with us for an extra week. We planned to do some sightseeing and enjoy more time together while they were in Ecuador. We decided to go to the coastal city of Manta and relax on the beach. After we hosted the church youth group for a week, we were exhausted.

We travelled seven hours by car from Quito to Manta. We were tired and hungry. The manager of the hotel directed us to a Chinese restaurant about a mile down the road. My daughter, Alesha, and her friend Kiegan decided to stay at the hotel because he was feeling sick. So, my three sons Derek, Philip, and Mathias jumped in two taxi cabs with Ben and Becky. They arrived at the Chinese restaurant at approximately 7:30 in the evening. After eating and paying the bill, we all walked outside to wave down two taxis and return to the hotel. The whole street, as far as I could see, was desolate. There wasn't a single person or car in sight.

I felt a little uneasy being there totally alone with five children after dark.

I said, "Let's all jog back to the hotel."

After jogging for a few minutes, I noticed three men coming out of the shipping port entrance our right side. The first man was smoking a cigarette. I realized we were about to be assaulted.

I yelled in a loud voice, "Everybody over to the left side!"

Immediately Derek and Ben ran to the left side of the median. Philip, Matthias, and Becky didn't hear me. They continued to run toward the three waiting men. Now we were only a hundred yards from them, and I realized I had to stay with the younger children. They were clueless of the danger that awaited them.

We were now less than fifty yards away from the men. The two teenage boys were on the far left side of the four-lane street, and the younger children were almost upon the three waiting men. I caught the eye of the man with the cigarette, and I raised fists like a man training for a boxing match would run. Our eyes locked in a stare-down. My eyes communicated that I knew what they were about to do and that I was prepared for a fight. All of this happened in a five- to ten-second period of time. I didn't take my eyes off the leader. At the last possible second, he backed down. We passed right by them without incident. I was very relieved and surprised.

I believe it confused them when Dereck and Ben flanked off to the left and intimidated them when I locked eyes with the leader. I also believe that God protected us from a potential assault that summer night many years ago.

He is a shield to all who trust in Him
(2 Samuel 22:31).

Chapter 12

Jungle Creatures

———————⟡⟡⟡———————

I will never forget the wonderful and solemn celebration the elders of the village of Kusutka gave me after the first two years of bringing the Gospel to them.

We gathered together under the thatched-roof community kitchen and dining hall. Several of the older village leaders gave serious and passionate speeches to me about how grateful they were that we had brought the Gospel of Christ to the jungle, and especially to Kusutka Village. After about fifteen minutes of these heart-felt proclamations of gratitude, the women brought out a two-quart container filled with a very special delicacy. As one of the women handed me the container, she let me know that of all the things they could offer me this was the greatest. She also made it very clear that it was *all* for me. Bon Appetite.

I felt deeply honored and very thankful for the treasured gift. Imagine my surprise when I took away the cover guarding the top of the two-quart gourd and saw about two-pounds of worms. There were long skinny ones, short fat ones, and everything in between.

All the men in unison said, "Eat up."

I knew I was between a rock and a hard place. My last two years of ministry were in danger of being lost, or at least tainted, if I didn't accept their most gracious and generous hospitality. It was the *best* they could offer. In an act of reckless abandon, I took one of the long slimy earthworms and let it slide down my throat without chewing it. Then I ate another. This act was purely by faith. All of a sudden, I had the most creative thought I've ever had in my life.

I said to the group of Shuar Indians gathered there, "I can honestly say I've never eaten anything quite like these worms in my life. Thank you, so, so much for this privilege. Thank you for sharing a very precious part of your culture with me. I appreciate it so much.

Now, I want to return the favor and share a part of my culture with you. In the United States if someone is especially blessed he shares that blessing with others. I would be making a pig of myself if I ate all these incredible worms without sharing them. I must share this wonderful blessing with all of you here."

You would have thought it was Christmas in July! Within minutes, all of worms were gone. I was delighted and very relieved.

The Lord had done it again. He didn't allow me to be tempted beyond my capacity. He gave me a way out from having to eat all those slimy worms. *No temptation has overtaken you except such as is common to man; but God is faithful, who will not allow you to be tempted beyond what you are able, but with the temptation will also make a way of escape, that you may be able to bear it* (1 Corinthians 10:13).

Another custom of the Shuar Indians is to go out at 3:00 a.m. during the full moon every April. That is when the flying ants leave the ground and fly two to five feet above the ground in large swarms. These ants are prized, because they have a sweet butter taste. They are eaten raw or roasted. Either way will do for the connoisseur of this fine delicacy. I have participated in the custom and eaten the ants. It's still not on my top ten favorite things to do. However, it is fun to take part in the festivities with the Shuar.

On the topic of interesting insects, during my first three years as a missionary in the jungle it was my practice to sleep on a hut floor. After I set up my air mattress and blanket I sprayed a circle of bug spray around my sleeping area. I prayed that no insect, tarantula, black scorpion, crab spider, or the likes would dare to venture across my "ring of fire" protection. It usually worked, but not this time.

About two weeks after a visit to the jungle, I noticed a large red lump on my upper left arm near my shoulder. It continued to grow larger and redder over the next several weeks.

Mission Aviation Fellowship pilot, Jim Manley, shared his opinion with me after I showed him the large red bump. "It looks like what my dog gets from time to time, but it doesn't have a hole in the top of it like he gets."

Well, a week later a hole formed in my large, red, pyramid-shaped lump. Following Jim's instructions, I squeezed out a large, fat, grub-like creature from my arm. It was about one inch long. I had given birth to a worm larva.

As bad as that experience was, there was good that came out of it. I can now relate on some level with the pains of childbirth that my wife Debbie experienced five times.

After this, I used mosquito nets to keep the insects and other creatures off me at night while I slept.

> *You therefore must endure hardship as a good soldier of Jesus Christ* (2 Timothy 2:3).

Chapter 13

Building Churches

⬥⬥⬥

In 1995, we began construction of the jungle church in the village of Kumai, located in the Pastaza Province. All was going according to plan with "Wild Bill" and Danny heading up the work, just as they had two years prior in Kusutka. I contracted a veteran Shuar woodcutter to cut the approximately one thousand boards we needed for the church building.

A month after I built the base, I returned with cement pylons and large wooden beams. We were ready to start work on the floor, walls, and roof. Much to my chagrin, as we started to measure the rough-cut boards it became obvious that *every* board was cut two to three inches under the standard agreed upon length of three meters (about ten feet).

I questioned the Shuar Indian woodcutter.

He smiled sheepishly and said, "I guess my measuring stick broke about ten centimeters (four inches)."

Whoops. What this meant was that the entire design with the ten-foot standard was useless. Everything had to be re-designed to accommodate the new shorter standard measurement of nine feet instead of ten. The floor, the walls, the roof, everything had to be re-designed to use the cut wood we had available. Wow!

After the shock, I became disoriented. Then denial set in. After that, anger and numbness. Acceptance came about twenty minutes later. Miraculously, I was able to somewhat hide my initial feelings of devastation and anger. I quickly executed Plan B. We followed the old World War II adage, "Do the best you can with what you've got."

Thank God, it all worked out fine. The church got built, and no one ever knew of the veteran wood cutter's big goof up.

The third church built was in the village of Kawa, also in the Pastaza province. It didn't have a landing strip in 1996. So, we flew to Kumai from Shell and walked with our supplies, food, and construction tools the three miles to Kawa.

My home church, Grace Assembly of God of Syracuse, NY, sent the funds and a construction team of seven men to build the Kawa church.

It was a highlight of my missionary career to have my own home church help with this deep-jungle church building project.

We landed in Kumai, got our gear together, and set off with several Shuar Indians to help carry supplies the three miles to Kawa. After a strenuous three-hour hike through the mountainous jungle with large backpacks, we all arrived safely but exhausted in Kawa.

The big surprise came next. There were no nails at the construction site in Kawa. Evidently, my message to send the one hundred pounds of nails never reached the right people at the Missions Aviation Fellowship hanger. The nails were still sitting in the storage room in Shell. We were forty miles away in the jungle with a construction team that was ready to work.

Again, as in the case of the one thousand short-cut boards in Kumai, I went through the full spectrum of emotions. Due to my sheer exhaustion from the eight-hour ride from Quito, the flight to Kumai, and then a grueling three-hour hike, my first reaction was despair. How can this be? I asked them three months ago to fly the nails, roofing materials, and gasoline to Kumai. Then I left instructions for the men of Kawa to carry them to the site for the building date.

At first I thought, *I can't do this. I don't have the strength or energy to walk back to radio MAF in Kumai and then return again to Kawa.* But I had no other choice. We couldn't do anything without the nails. Fortunately, we brought ten pounds of extra nails. The men could at least get started. So after about forty-five minutes of recuperation, I set out by myself to return to Kumai.

On my way back from Kumai late in the afternoon, I stumbled along in complete exhaustion when an x-snake slithered over my boot. My adrenaline shocked me into an alerted state. I jumped back and almost fell over. I struck the deadly snake and killed it. It could have bit me with its fatal poison. To make matters worse, I was by myself. I thanked God for His divine protection and giving me the strength I needed to make the difficult six-mile round trip when I thought it would have been impossible. The nails came, the church got built, and we lived through it to tell another story.

I can do all things through Christ, who strengthens me (Philippians 4:13).

Chapter 14

Three Deaths on the Same Day

—————❖❖❖—————

April 15, 2008, will be forever remembered in the jungle village of Kuakash. It was the day three people from their village died. Albeit, in three different places.

The first to die was a young, two-year-old boy named Chiriap. He had been sick for several months and died in the village itself.

The second to die was a nineteen-year-old girl in a hospital outside the jungle in Ambato. She also had been sick for some time and died from a long and painful infection.

The third person to die that day was a thirty-three-year-old man named Marco Ankuash. He was a husband and father of four children. He had also been the director of my Christian High School in the village. Marco died of a fatal heart attack while staying at a hotel in the jungle town of Puyo. This was the most unexpected death. By all appearances, he seemed to be the picture of health and vitality.

The significant part of this story was the extreme and unforeseen reaction the village had after these three deaths in one day.

I arrived in their village a week later. The grief and shock was palpable. For two days we taught, prayed, and exhorted the

Shuar Indians of Kuakash to look to Christ for healing, comfort, and peace in the midst of these devastating events. When I had to leave, I didn't feel a peace in my heart that the village was coping well yet. There seemed to be something going on that I couldn't put my finger on, but I had to leave to tend to matters in other villages. On top of all this, I was only weeks away from our year-long furlough in the states.

I asked Pastor Jorge Ailla if he would please go to Kuakash and spend some more time with them. I still had no peace leaving them alone. God's wisdom, timing, and power was so incredible in this situation.

Several days later when Pastor Jorge arrived in Kuakash, he was shocked to see a witchdoctor among the villagers. The witchdoctor was invited by the non-Christian village leaders to determine who was to blame for the deaths a week earlier.

When Pastor Jorge saw this desperate situation, he went to the church and fell on his face before God and cried out in prayer for mercy and help. After two hours, he felt a powerful peace in his heart. He went out to discover that the villagers had kicked out the witchdoctor. The people were at peace with the deaths and with one another.

The reason the expulsion of the witchdoctor was so, so, so, important was this: If he stayed and somehow determined someone was to blame for the three deaths, that person or family would be put to death immediately to avenge the three deaths the week prior.

From that point on, there would have been continuous vengeance deaths. The blamed one's relatives would put to death those they suspected of tipping off the witchdoctor. On and on it would go; blaming and killing, avenging, and killing again.

All of that was prevented by Pastor Jorge's hours of earnest prayer before he ever spoke a word to the villagers.

Have respect to the covenant; For the dark places of the earth are full of the haunts of cruelty. Oh, do not let the oppressed return ashamed! Let the poor and needy praise your name (Psalm 74:20-21).

Chapter 15

Teen Challenge Vision in Ecuador

———— ✧✦✧ ————

D ebbie and I were appointed as foreign missionaries with the Assemblies of God in 1986. We never imagined being involved with starting a Teen Challenge. Teen Challenge is a Christian rehab founded by Rev. David Wilkerson in 1958. Our calling to serve in Ecuador included Evangelistic Tent Campaigns and Jungle Ministry. However, after preaching and teaching in the prison for several years, the Lord spoke to my heart about starting a Teen Challenge in Ecuador.

When Ecuadorian Jorge Ailla finished his two-year sentence for financial troubles in his business, he began to work with newly released prisoners in his carpentry shop. In April 1995, we rented a house in North Quito and had twelve men in our newly formed Teen Challenge. For the next two years, this is how we ministered to men with drug and alcohol addictions. The vast majority of these men were recently released prisoners. This was not the case in the Syracuse Teen Challenge. Only about 20%-30% of those men had served jail or prison time.

After a year and a half, Jorge mentioned to me that an Ecuadorian widow was selling her property. It was almost two acres for $70,000. He suggested we buy it to expand our Teen Challenge ministry.

At first, I absolutely refused to even consider such a project. I was so involved with other activities at the time I couldn't even think of what this expansion would involve. Soon, my area director, Norm Campbell, approached me with $5,000 seed money to purchase the property. I still didn't want to agree to what I felt would be an overwhelming amount of stress and work without the needed financial backing. However, I did agree to pray about it just to get them off my back. Within two weeks, I was convinced that the Lord wanted a large Teen Challenge Ministry. I put the seed money down as a non-refundable down payment.

Next came the many days of letter writing, phone calls, faxes, and sleepless nights. I prayed for the $65,000 to come in five months so that we wouldn't lose the property and the $5000 deposit. We signed the notarized contract on August 31, 1996. I had until January 31, 1997, to have the full $70,000 in the widow's account.

After more than four months of intense fund raising and prayer, we still lacked $40,000. We only had two weeks left to fulfill the agreement or lose the deposit and the property.

Satan attacked me by placing doubtful words and thoughts in my mind as I walked the halls of the house during the nighttime hours. *Shame on you for presuming to hear from God concerning this fool's errand. Many good Christian people have put their trust in you for this project. You will disappoint them. You will fail and lose everything. What a travesty. What a great shame on you.*

This bombardment of discouraging and accusing thoughts dominated my mind for weeks. Now it was to the point where it was almost unbearable. My only temporary relief was crying out to God in prayer and asking for a miracle.

After a horrific night of gloom and despair, I received a phone call from the States. It was evangelist Steve Hill of the Brownsville Revival in Pensacola, Florida. He received my fax months prior, as did other pastors. I didn't know him and he didn't know me.

His first question right off the bat was, "Tim, how is your fundraising going for the Teen Challenge Property in Ecuador?"

I responded by faith, "It's going great. We have $30,000 raised so far."

"How much time do you have?"

"Two weeks."

"How much do you need?"

"Forty thousand dollars."

Steve replied, "I'm going to make a few phone calls and cover that. You can get some rest now."

Wow. I have never before or since had such a large amount given all at once. And I have never felt the weight of stress and demonic attack lift from me so suddenly. Steve made three phone calls. The money was raised quickly. All $70,000 was in the account on the designated day, January 31, 1997. It was not there one day before or one day after. Jesus put His seal of approval on the project by providing the funds at *exactly* the time needed to fulfill a notarized document.

> *My times are in Your hand. Deliver me from the hand of my enemies, and from those who persecute me. Do not let me be ashamed, O Lord, for I have called upon you* (Psalm 31:15, 17).

Tim and Debbie Wedding Day, July 2nd, 1983

Tim and Debbie, with First Child, Alesha

First Prayer Card, 1986

Derek, Alesha, and Philip

Anderson Prayer Card, 1997

Alesha and Abby, 2000

Zac, Our Dog

Zoey, Our 220 lb. Neapolitan Mastiff

Our Five Kids Up in the Mountains

Alesha, Philip, and Derek with Our First Dog, Charity

Anderson Family, 2009

Harry Sharples, Tim's Mentor

Our Three Sons in Dress Blues, USAF

Anderson Family, 2016

Debbie, the Greatest Missionary Wife Ever!

Debbie's Father, the Honorable
Orm Gale (County Court Judge)

Debbie's Mother, Jo Gale

Tim's Parents, Kathleen and Don, First Row
Brothers Peter, Tim, and Rand, Back Row

Tim's Father, Don Anderson, Pilot in USAF

Church Service in Kuakash, 1994

Church Service in Kuakash, In New Church Building

Church Service in Kusutka

Dr. Mike Vaughn Doing Chiropractic Adjustments in the Jungle

Dr. Ron Lamb During Jungle Medical Clinic

First Bible School Graduates in Riobamba, Ecuador

First Jungle Church, Kusutka, 1993

Grace Assembly of God Men's Mission Trip
to Build Kawa Church in the Jungle

Tim and Pablo

Pastor Onelio and Tim at a Jungle Water Baptism Service

Pastor Onelio and Tim Praying After a Water Baptism Service at the River

Prayer in the Kawa Jungle Church

Really Only a 100 lb. Balsom Wood Log!

Samuel and Gonsalo Eating on Palm Leaves

Second Jungle Church in Kumai, 1994

Shuar Ladies Praying in Kumai

The Old Voz Andes Hospital in Shell, Ecuador

Third Jungle Church in Kawa, 1996

Tim and Jorge with Jungle Leaders in Kawa

Tim and Onelio at Water Baptism Service in Jungle River of Kusutka

Tim at Jungle Water Baptism in Kusutka

Tim Giving Instructions Before Water Baptism Service in Jungle

Tim Praying for Healing in Campamiento Ayuy Village

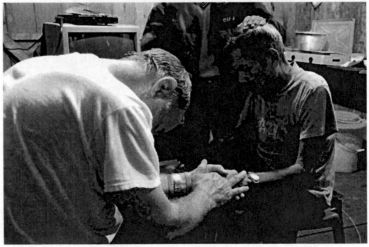

Tim Praying with Shuar Man Luis in Kumai

Tim Preaching at Church Service

Tim with a Boa Constrictor, Before Flying Into Jungle

Tim Unpacking the MAF Plane in the Jungle

Typical Jungle Hut in the Morona Santiago Province

Alonso and Luis Ready to Climb Papallacta Mountain with Tim, 1990

Andean Area Directors Norm and Mary ann Campell

Calvary's Love Chuch in South Quito

Grace Assembly and Trinity Assembly Youth Missions Team

Men's Prison Courtyard During Evangelism Outreach

Putting Up the Tent

First Tent Campaign in El Inca, 1989

Tent Campaign, 1990

Tim Preaching in San Francisco Plaza, Quito

Youth Missions Team in Our 1981 (Speed the Light) Chevy Blazer

Don Wilkerson Speaking at Teen Challenge, with Tim Translating

Ecuador Teen Challenge with Students and Staff

Ecuador Teen Challenge, 2016

The Visiting Area of Ecuador Teen Challenge

Tim Presenting a Graduation Plaque to a Student

Prayer Time at a Teen Challenge Graduation

Tim with Teen Challenge Staff

Teen Challenge Group Picture

Chapter 16

Gonzalo's Amazing Conversion

———————— ✕◈✕ ————————

I was told of the village of Kusutka when I first started going into the deep southern jungles of Ecuador. Some suggested I minister there, because no one had visited there with the Gospel of Christ.

A man named Gonzalo really stood out. He was in his mid-thirties and wore his hair long, as is the custom of the Ashuar Indians. The Ashuar are cousins of the Shuar.

Gonzalo came to the church services at night, when I preached. He sat there with his arms crossed in utter defiance and with resistance written all over his face. Yet, he kept coming. This went on for a full five years during my monthly visits to the jungle.

In 1993, I began a Master's Degree with Asuza Pacific University in California. The professors came to Quito, Ecuador, every year for forty hours of instruction during a two-week period. One of my classes was called Crossing Cultural Barriers. Part of the work in this particular class required me to go into the home of someone from another culture and ask them forty questions concerning the particulars of their culture.

God used this course to prompt me to ask Gonzalo if I could come into his hut and ask him interesting and revealing questions regarding the customs of the Shuar Indians living deep in the jungle. He agreed. I learned so much about the Shuar community and Gonzalo himself. He was very proud of his heritage and nation. He also opened up to me about a horrible nightmare he had several years prior.

In Gonzalo's dream, he was tormented by two demons who clung viciously to his heart. No matter what he tried to do to pry them off, they would not let go. Later in the dream, a man walked up to him and hugged him in a strong embrace. When the man hugged him the two tormenting demons fell off, and he felt great freedom and peace.

He went on to say, "Hermano Timoteo, tu eres, el hombre en mi sueño que me abrazo." (Brother Tim, you are the man in my dream that came and hugged me).

I was shocked. However, in the next several months I noticed a big difference in Gonzalo. Soon, he came forward during the invitation to receive Christ as his Savior in front of his whole village.

Satan tries to prevent us from giving our lives wholly to Christ. Thankfully, God has the last word and knows how to reach into our hearts and defeat the demonic strongholds that keep us captive. Hallelujah!

> *For behold, the darkness shall cover the earth, and deep darkness the people; but the Lord will arise over you, and His glory will be seen upon you* (Isaiah 60:2).

Chapter 17

Divine Delay

In April of 2009, we decided to sell the Teen Challenge car. It was a 1994 Suzuki hatch back that started to cost more in repairs than it was worth. Even with the age of the car and the many miles on it, we were able to find a buyer willing to pay $3000.

Under recently changed Ecuadorian law, both the husband and the wife had to sign the necessary documents for the transaction. The buyer agreed to meet at my house at 12:15 p.m. for Debbie and me to sign the documents and receive the $3000.

My sub-director of Teen Challenge, Ivan Suin, agreed to attend the meeting and bring the title of the car to complete the sale. The Suzuki car would remain at Teen Challenge for several days until all the necessary paper work was completed, and the car was legally transferred and registered.

I was coming from HCJB radio station in Quito, and Debbie would leave school shortly after noon to meet for the signing at 12:15 p.m. That was the plan. We are both normally punctual and knew this meeting was important. Things did not go as planned. Debbie and I were both delayed by about five minutes.

When we arrived late, Ivan's face was white with fear. Then he told us what just happened.

The buyer went to his bank to withdraw the $3000 in cash to buy the car. Evidently, he was being watched and then followed to my house. Upon arriving with the cash in hand, five well-armed thieves stole the buyer's $3000 cash and his car. If Debbie and I had arrived five minutes earlier, I hate to think of what could have happened. Our car could have been stolen and we may have been kidnapped as well. Thank God for His divine delay to avert a disastrous and traumatic event in our lives.

A man's steps are of the Lord; How then can a man understand his own way? (Proverbs 20:24).

Chapter 18

Power over Demons

The early years of the 1980's were full of intense spiritual warfare ministry. One powerful lesson came through three prayer sessions. The first prayer session was with my Pastor, Arvin Sorge, at my home church, Grace Assembly of God in Syracuse, NY. Pastor Sorge and I ministered to a young man who asked for prayer. During the prayer time, we felt a strong desire to proclaim the blood of Christ over him. He reacted violently.

After several minutes, a deep, guttural voice came out of him saying, "Don't say the blood of Jesus, it's burning me like fire."

What a surprise. Of course, we proclaimed the blood of Jesus over that young man all the more. Soon, the demons left him and he was set free. That experience left a great impression on me as a young minister.

After several more months, while I prayed with the men at Syracuse Teen Challenge, the same thing happened again.

We prayed over one of the Teen Challenge students when a deep voice came from him.

It said, "Do not say that word."

I asked, "What word?"

The demon replied, "The *blood!* Don't say that word. It burns us like fire."

This was the second time within just a few months where two different people in different places reacted in this manner. From then on, it became my practice to always proclaim the Blood of Christ while praying for others, for myself, for divine protection, and every night over my family before we went to bed. It is the place of eternal victory for Jesus and eternal defeat for Satan. I always go to the blood before all else. It is the divine standard by which God judges sin, the world, and Satan. *They overcame him (Satan) by the Blood of the Lamb and by the word of their testimony* (Revelation 12:11). My desire is to have His blood continually cover my loved ones and myself. There is "wonder working power in the blood."

Another spiritual warfare lesson from that same time came from a young man called Bob. He had been a Syracuse Teen Challenge student. He returned to his apartment in a rough area on Syracuse's west side after only staying a few days. Bob and I kept in contact over the next several years. I kept trying to minister the grace of God to him. He had a lot of deep-seated problems and had been in and out of the psychiatric hospital and jail during that time.

One Sunday afternoon, I went to visit Bob and take him to Sunday evening church at Grace Assembly. My only requirements were that he not come to church on drugs or drunk. When I got to his house, I could tell that he had been drinking by the foul odor of his breath.

I said, "I told you not to drink before going to church."

I was angry and frustrated with him for not keeping his word.

"Brother Tim, I only had a little. Please let me go to church with you."

"All right," I finally agreed, "you better have only had a little." Off to church we went.

It was my custom to arrive an hour before the night service and pray downstairs in the Sunday school rooms. Bob and I knelt down to pray. I lifted up my hands and started to worship the Lord. Bob followed suit by lifting his hands as well. What came out of his mouth next was *not* worship. A deep roar came from the depths of Bob's being, then another. He quickly stood up and grabbed eight-foot tables and threw them across the room. Here I was, alone with a violent, demon-possessed man in the basement of my church. It wouldn't be the last time either.

I stood up and looked straight at Bob and yelled in a loud voice, "You overpowering demon, I bind you in the name of the Lord Jesus Christ!"

Bob dropped to the floor like a sack of potatoes, flat onto his back.

Again, a deep, raspy voice came out of him, saying, "I am the all-powerful one."

At that point, a friend of mine, Ron, with experience in spiritual warfare, came in to help me, as if on cue by God Himself.

I said to the demon, who called himself the Macedonian, "So if you are the all-powerful one, why are you lying on the floor under the power of Jesus' name?"

It was at that moment that I understood why Satan was referred to as the *father of lies*. His underlings also live by this great self-delusion. Even though this demon was helpless under Jesus' authority, he kept believing he was all powerful. I thought, *Satan's twisted and unrealistic frame of reference is ludicrous in the face of the obvious reality.* He really is brain damaged since his defeat at Calvary's cross. Ron and I prayed for Bob, and he came out of his demon-controlled state. The alcohol and his sinful lifestyle gave the enemy easy access to Bob. This lesson prompted me to covenant with the Holy Spirit to never drink any alcohol that could possibly give the enemy a foothold in my life. I have kept this covenant for forty years now and will keep it until death.

> *It is not for kings to drink wine, nor for princes*
> *intoxicating drink; lest they drink and forget the*
> *law, and pervert the justice of all the afflicted*
> (Proverbs 31:4-5).

Chapter 19

Giant Anacondas

—◇◇◇—

O ver the last thirty years, I have heard dozens of incredible snake stories from those who encountered the dangerous reptiles deep in Ecuador's Amazon. Most of these stories are of the giant anaconda whose legendary and mythical status increases with the years. The three stories I am about to tell, as far as I know, are true. The people who shared them with me are credible and have nothing to gain by lying.

Northern Jungle Village

Near the Northern jungle town of Lago Agrio there is a restaurant next to a primitive zoo. Some years ago, as I travelled in that area to minister to the Cofan Indians with fellow missionaries Rick and Ron Borman, I stopped in the restaurant and made friends with the owner, Carlos. He told me the most amazing story.

One of the indigenous tribes in the area asked him to come to their rescue. A giant anaconda invaded their village, and they feared for their lives. Upon his arrival, he saw the huge swath the snake made on the ground as it entered and left the village. Carlos found the reptile in the hut of one of the villagers. The snake was sedentary because it had just eaten a big meal. Carlos took his shotgun and shot the snake in the head. It was dead. He took his large knife and slit open the snake's bulging belly. What he saw sickened him. Inside the snake, he discovered a dead woman, her child and two full-grown jungle deer. He didn't mention the exact size of the snake – or if he did, I've forgotten. The details of what he found in the snake's belly are precise, and he told them to me personally with great conviction and sadness.

The Anaconda and the Tourists

This story was from the former director of my jungle high school, the president of the village of Kuakash. He was also the thirty-three-year-old man who died on the same day as two others from his village in April of 2008. His name was Marco Ankuash.

In his early twenties, Marco was a tour guide on the Napo River in the Amazon region of Ecuador. The river runs near the town of Tena then heads east deep into the jungle. He was a knowledgeable guide and very familiar with the region, including animal habitat, the dangerous areas, the currents of the rivers, and daily torrential Amazon rains.

Marco and the twelve tourists with him rounded the bend in the river. They were aghast to see one of the largest creatures on planet Earth.

As they passed by the sandy beach, a gigantic anaconda was curled up in the warm afternoon sun. They were all amazed. When I asked Marco to describe the length of the snake, he only shook his head.

He said, "We could not tell how long the snake was because he was curled up tight. We couldn't even see its head, but we could see how *thick* it was."

He indicated that the thickness of the snake's body was equal to his height. Marco was a 5-foot 8-inch full-grown man. I was stunned. I repeated the question several times to make sure I understood him correctly. Each time he described the same scene verbally and by indicating with his hand.

Marco told me the tourists took photographs of the sleeping snake as they passed by in their canoe. However, they were so frightened that they continued several more miles downstream to find a campsite for the night. They were all so distraught that none of them were able to sleep for fear that the creature would attack them during the night.

They returned the next morning to the place they saw the anaconda. It was gone. All that remained of the great serpent was the large undulating path in the sand that led back into the river. This was a jungle tour neither Marco nor his tourists would ever forget.

Marco had nothing to gain by lying or exaggerating. I still found it very difficult to believe, until I heard a similar snake story from Africa. Just because we have never seen or heard of something, doesn't mean it doesn't exist.

The Anaconda and the Canoe

This story took place fifteen years ago on the Canambo River near the Peruvian Border in Ecuador's jungle. Missionary Chis Ranalli's father, Albert, enjoyed hunting large tapirs for fresh meat. The indigenous tribes forced them out of their hiding places with their spears and dogs. Then the tapirs jumped into the river to escape the dogs, only to be shot by Albert.

Unwittingly, the natives roused a giant anaconda that had just killed and swallowed a big tapir. The snake moved sluggishly, desperate to get away from the spears and the dogs. Albert saw the giant snake slither into the river and got a shot off.

"I must have missed it," he exclaimed in frustration.

In the next few seconds, the huge snake closed the distance between itself and Albert's canoe. It came up under the small canoe and quickly wrapped itself around the boat several times. It was about to bite Albert when his survival instinct took over. He shot the behemoth in the mouth, through the brain, and instantly killed it. That was the story behind the twenty-two-foot snake skin stretched across their wall with the two bullet holes in it. The first hole in the snake skin is in the middle, where it was shot entering the river. The second shot went through its head during the attack. That was not Hollywood. *That* was jungle survival.

Chapter 20

Amazing Survival

—◇◇◇—

In the early years of Ecuador Teen Challenge, the vast majority of our students came directly from prison or from the
streets. This was a very rough cross-section of society that survived for a while and then usually died violently. As they lived,
so they died, or killed others trying to survive.

Jimmy Acosta spent many years in the Men's Prison #2 when
he was a young man. Later, he was sent to the Men's Maximum
Security Prison in Quito, Ecuador, as the seriousness and violence of his crimes escalated. That prison was Garcia Moreno.
After serving his sentence of six years, Jimmy came into our
center for a period of months, though he didn't complete the
full program.

Little did we realize at the time, but my co-founder of
Ecuador Teen Challenge would come close to giving his life for
the cause of Christ. Only by the grace of God was Jorge able to
endure "the night from hell."

At that time, Jorge was my sub-director. He lived on the Teen
Challenge compound by himself in a small two-bedroom house.

A wall stood between his house and the main Teen Challenge building. About one hundred feet separated the two buildings.

That night, Jorge prepared to go to bed and Jimmy waited in the darkness. Jimmy was in a drug-crazed rage and intended to kill Jorge Ailla that night.

Jimmy attacked. He cut Jorge's arms but wasn't able to plunge the knife into his chest to finish him off. This demon-possessed man tried for more than six hours to kill Jorge. In those dark overnight hours, he did a lot of physical damage to Jorge. None of the other leaders or students heard the two men struggle. As day broke, they finally heard Jorge call for help in a low hoarse voice. Before the staff and students could come to Jorge's rescue, Jimmy ran from the Teen Challenge property, jumped over the wall, and escaped.

Jorge was taken to the hospital. He had deep gashes on his forearm and bicep in addition to numerous chest wounds. A plastic surgeon stitched Jorge back together free of charge. As far as we know, Jorge never suffered any permanent psychological trauma and was able to forgive Jimmy for his vicious and murderous attack. And Jimmy knew deep down that Jorge had only been trying to help him.

Jimmy would go on to live a wild, drug-filled life that involved being in and out of prison many times in the next seventeen years. He eventually showed back up at Teen Challenge, many years later, to seek forgiveness from Jorge. Jorge freely gave it to him.

God used this incident to establish Teen Challenge in our Barrio of Marianas. The town was determined to drive Teen Challenge out before the attempted murder. They feared all the dangerous men we had at the center. Within days of Jorge's near death experience, the whole town turned out in a wonderful show of love and support for Jorge. Even the local Catholic priest, who was opposed to our ministry, came to give an offering and pray for Jorge. From that point forward, there were no more attempts to throw Teen Challenge out of the village. The ministry was established.

> *All things work together for good for those who love God, to those who are called according to His Purpose* (Romans 8:28).

Chapter 21

Long Walks, Talks, and Dreams in the Jungle

———⫸⟨✕⟩⫷———

Some of the most interesting and informative times of my life have been hiking from village to village with my young Shuar Indian guides. The time spent on the muddy jungle paths provided me with the unique opportunity to learn about the culture, legends, myths, customs, and spiritual world of the Shuar people.

In the spring of 2003, I visited my hub-village of Kusutka for three days. After I finished my time there, I planned to hike three hours to the Pastaza River. I would cross the river by canoe and continue another two hours to Kuakash, in the Pastaza Province. This is normally a five-hour trip.

The trek is exhausting, because there are numerous rises and falls in this particular part of the jungle. The most demanding and dangerous leg of the journey is, by far, climbing down the 400-foot cliff which brings you down into the Pastaza River Valley. It is steep, slippery, and in some places without anything to keep you from falling to the bottom. I always take extra caution and pray continually while traversing this route.

A Shuar Indian in his early twenties was my guide on this particular trip from Kusutka to Kuakash. His name was Galo. We walked and talked for three hours while approaching the huge river. Galo told me about diabolical dreams he had over the last several years.

He said, "At night in my hut, there was a large, dark figure who kept saying he would kill me, my wife, and child."

He was terrified by this but didn't know what to make of it or what to do about it. Witchcraft and witchdoctors are prevalent in the jungle. This was the perfect time to talk about spiritual matters. I told him of Christ's tremendous power and desire to protect him and his family from satanic attacks.

As we talked, a great hunger for God came over Galo. We prayed and he received Jesus Christ as his Savior. The Holy Spirit gave him a wonderful peace and confidence that God would keep him and his family safe from whatever traps or schemes the enemy had in mind. That happened more than thirteen years ago as of the writing of this book.

On August 3, 2012, Galo and I walked together again. This time it was a four-hour hike from Kuakash to Chapintza. He told me of his recent dreams about traveling to the United States and seeing the big cities like New York City.

In this dream there was a very large angel who said to him, "If you are to see the United States, you must prepare yourself to be very strong in the Lord. You cannot enter it without being very strong and prepared."

I thought to myself how interesting it was that he would have dreams of a trip to the United States from the deep jungles of Ecuador. God was saying *if* you are to go, you must be prepared and strong spiritually. It's interesting how Biblical this experience of Galo's is. *And it shall come to pass afterward that I will pour out my Spirit on all flesh, your sons and daughters shall prophesy, your old men shall dream dreams, your young men shall see visions. And also on My menservants and on My maid-servants I will pour out my Spirit in those days* (Joel 2:28-29).

Galo has been one of the Christian professors at our evangelical high school in Kuakash for the last two years. He maintains a good testimony in his village as well as with his family. Who knows, perhaps one day he will see his dreams fulfilled and visit the United States. One thing is sure, Galo *will* be strong in Christ and well-prepared for the trip. He may be going to evangelize many people right in New York City. If it was just a dream of his own imagination, we will know soon enough.

Chapter 22

The High-Octane Fuel of the Jungle

———⟨⟩⟨⟩———

Many, many times I have suffered extreme thirst in the jungle as I travelled from one village to another. I have used all sorts of ways to stay hydrated, including iodine pills to treat river water, portable water filters, and Camel Back water backpacks.

The way the Shuar Indians stay hydrated and strong for the countless miles of hiking through the hot, muddy, and mountainous terrain of the jungles of Ecuador is all summed up in one word. CHICHA.

Chicha is a thick, oatmeal-textured drink derived from the yucca root. It's boiled until soft. Then the women of the tribe chew on it to mix it with their saliva and spit it into a pot to mix with water. The fibers are filtered out by hand and voila. If it's allowed to sit several days, it becomes fermented and has an alcohol content similar to wine or beer. It's against my convictions to drink alcohol, so I have only ever consumed fresh Chicha.

I noticed how the Shuar men drank large amounts of it when

we walked between villages. It seemed to refresh and invigorate them. Several years ago, I was in our main village of Kusutka with a Missionary Associate from the Assemblies of God, Joe Hewes, and Ecuadorian Pastor, Diego Ushina. We needed to hike to the village of Timias approximately three hours from Kusutka. It was a hot day, and to make matters worse, we started our hike in the late morning when the sun was already out. The temperature rose rapidly. Joe and I realized we hadn't packed enough water for the six-hour round trip.

When we arrived in Timias to visit the Latin American Child Care (LACC) school and update the student records, we both felt very tired and dehydrated. Some women offered me a quart-size bowl of Chicha, and I accepted it gladly. I drank two full bowls in just a few minutes. On our return trip to Kusutka, I felt a surge of energy and vitality. I ran through the jungle with speed and endurance, and leaped like a gazelle over the fallen logs and tree roots. The Chicha dramatically affected my physical and mental condition in an amazing way. I returned to Kusutka with energy to spare.

Unfortunately, I also contracted the Giardia parasite. The Chicha I drank was made with contaminated river water. It was a very miserable two months for me to get the right medicine and clean out my system from that awful parasite. For that reason, I have sworn off drinking the "high octane fuel of the jungle." Yet, I still recall with fond memories the strength and energy of that almost magical drink. Chicha provided me with energy, stamina, and hydration. It helped me survive and thrive under the very demanding conditions of walking between villages on the Amazon jungle paths.

The last thirty years has been a battle between staying hydrated and avoiding parasites. Many times the water is fine, and I don't come down with amoebas or parasites. Other times I do. I've had to choose either to hydrate and risk contracting a parasite or not hydrate and risk my body shutting down in the middle of the jungle. The latter is far more dangerous. All in all, God has been very good to us, protected us, and helped us survive and fulfill His purposes these many years deep in the Amazon Rain Forest.

> *Therefore we also, since we are surrounded by so great a cloud of witnesses, let us lay aside every weight, and the sin which so easily ensnares us, and let us **run with endurance** the race that is set before us, looking unto Jesus, the author and finisher of our faith, who for the joy that was set before Him endured the cross, despising its shame, and has sat down at the right hand of the throne of God* (Hebrews 12:1-2, emphasis added).

Chapter 23

God of Precision

———— ✦✦ ————

In October of 2010, Pastor Jorge Ailla and I flew into the jungle from the town of Shell, Ecuador. He visited the jungle village of Kuakash in the Pastaza Province. I flew into the village of Kusutka in the Morona Santiago Province. We were separated by the Pastaza River, a large tributary of the Amazon River, and a five-hour hike through the jungle. We remained in our respective villages for three days before hiking out on different routes. We had absolutely no contact for those three days. Our plan was to see each other back in Quito just in case one of us had trouble hiking out.

My hike was an eight-hour hike to the nearest dirt road and bus stop. Then I faced a three-hour bus ride to Puyo. After those legs of the trip, I had a ten-minute taxi ride from Puyo's bus terminal to where my car was parked at the airplane hangar in Shell. Once I got in the car, I faced a five-hour drive from Shell back up into two-mile-high Quito.

Jorge had a three-hour hike from Kuakash to Chipintza. Then he had a three-hour bus ride to Puyo. Once in Puyo, he also had the ten-minute taxi ride to Shell.

After we spent time in our respective villages, we left at *different times* to hike our way out. Jorge and I arrived **simultaneously** in Shell at the airport hangar. He arrived in a bus, and I arrived in a truck-taxi at precisely the same moment. Our jaws dropped in utter astonishment at how God ordered every step to orchestrate our arrival. I still stand amazed as I ponder the chances of that ever happening without divine intervention.

The Lord shall preserve your going out and your coming in from this time forth, and even forevermore (Psalm 121:8).

Chapter 24

A Week like No Other

―――――◇×◇――――――

Pastor Diego Ushina and I traveled from Quito to Shell
around midday on November 9, 2012. Independent airplane pilot, Rick LaBouff, flew us into the jungle village of
Kusutka at 4:00 p.m. The weather was perfect and everything
went smoothly.

The next day we attended a multi-village conference to
discuss some pending issues related to missionaries and the
Shuar people. It was a long, nine-hour meeting. A lot of pas-
sions and opinions were discussed in the 140-person gather-
ing. Thankfully, it ended on a good note. Pastor Diego and I
flew back late that day to Shell and drove the five hours back
to Quito, arriving around midnight.

Three days later, I noticed that I didn't feel well during a
Tuesday morning meeting at my apartment with two other missionaries and an Ecuadorian pastor. By night time, I felt down-
right miserable with nausea and deep aching pain throughout
my whole body. I couldn't sleep at all that night.

That same evening, Debbie and I both had our stool and
blood tested at a local medical clinic. It confirmed that I had

a severe bacterial infection in my intestines. We went to the emergency room at the Metropolitan Hospital in Quito. The resident doctor prescribed a strong prescription for the infection as well as pain medication for the next several days. By this time, I was experiencing intense pain and nausea as well as a fever and chills.

At 2:30 a.m. Wednesday morning, Debbie and I went to a 24-hour major chain pharmacy to fill the prescription, so I could begin treatment. Unfortunately, the pain medication's name was very similar to a strong anti-parasite medication that was also sold there. We didn't realize that the pharmacist gave us the *wrong* medicine. I was taking a high dosage of the wrong drug. This caused devastating and painful reactions within my body.

Along with the symptoms I was already experiencing, the strong dosage of anti-parasite drug caused additional symptoms like swelling of the liver, loss of appetite and dehydration. After several more sleepless nights and days of pain, I started having panic attacks and difficulty breathing. These became so unbearable that I checked back into the hospital two more times during the next four days.

For the first time in my life, I felt utter desperation to the point that thoughts of suicide became commonplace. I struggled minute by minute to survive. This went on for hours on end. The medical staff at the hospital completely downplayed my dilemma. I have never felt so desperate, helpless, and utterly distressed. To make matters worse, they didn't take me seriously. They thought I made it all up. Only Debbie knew what was going on with me. She was the only thing that kept me sane after eight days and nights with no sleep and severe pain.

A clinic doctor finally discovered the mistake the pharmacist made and confirmed the utter trauma I was experiencing. My mind, body, and spirit were derailed by a chemical imbalance in my body, and I still had the dangerous infection in my intestines. After eight days of extreme pain, fever, chills, no rest, no food, and a fatal level of dehydration, the severity of my situation became clear. My body was shutting down.

The entire time, I cried out to God for His healing and a way out of this unbearable situation. I lost *twenty pounds* in eight days. The demand on my heart and lungs was incredible. If not for my strong physical condition due to mountain climbing, I believe I could have died from a heart attack from the extreme strain on my body and internal organs.

It has now been four weeks since the experience. My body and mind still feel the effects of the strange chemical imbalance caused by combining wrong medications. I am still aware of the general fatigue caused by recovering from the bacterial infection. I feel greatly blessed to have survived this unusual ordeal. I'm also grateful for the brokenness and empathy God has put *in me* for others who struggle with chemical imbalances. Truly, I felt as if I was put through the "deep waters" of suffering and torment. I recognize it may pale in comparison to what many others go through who experience chronic pain and suffering. Yet, this experience has served a good purpose in me. Lord willing, I will not soon forget it or fail to apply my deeper care for others in their distress and helplessness.

> *For we do not want you to be ignorant, brethren,*
> *of our trouble which came to us in Asia* (Ecuador):
> *that we were burdened beyond measure, above*
> *strength, **so that we despaired even of life**. Yes,*
> *we had the sentence of death in ourselves, that we*
> *should not trust in ourselves but in God who raises*
> *the dead, who delivered us from so great a death,*
> *and does deliver us; in whom we trust that He will*
> *still deliver us, you also helping together in prayer*

for us, that thanks may be given by many persons on our behalf for the gift granted to us through many (2 Corinthians 1:8-11, emphasis added).

And He said to me, "My grace is sufficient for you, for My strength is made perfect in weakness." Therefore, most gladly I will rather boast in my infirmities, **that the power of Christ may rest upon.** *Therefore, I take pleasure in infirmities, in reproaches, in needs, in persecutions, in distresses, for Christ's sake. For when I am weak, then I am strong* (2 Corinthians 12:9-10, emphasis added).

Therefore let him who thinks he stands take heed lest he fall. No temptation has overtaken you except such as is common to man; but God is faithful, who will **not** *allow you to be tempted beyond what you are able, but with the temptation will also make the way of escape, that you may be able to bear it* (1 Corinthians 10:12-13, emphasis added).

Chapter 25

When the Holy Spirit Shouted

———— ✧✧ ————

In June of 1990, Debbie and I along with Pastor Arturo Espinel and his wife, Rosa, led an evangelistic tent campaign in Quito, Ecuador. This campaign continued seven nights per week for two years. We were there at least five nights per week. Arturo, Debbi, and I shared the responsibility of preaching and leading worship.

The phone in our house rang at about 1:00 p.m. that Thursday in June. It was Yolanda. She was the secretary for Paul Hutsell, our boss and the Andean Area Director of the five northernmost countries in South America. She received a call from a man named Scott, an American tourist visiting Quito for vacation. He told her he attended an Assembly of God church in the Baltimore, Maryland, area.

His story to Yolanda and us was, while he toured Quito, he encountered thieves who ran after him to rob him. In the ensuing chase, he fell two stories from an upper street to a lower one and broke his leg. He was in one of the local hospitals recovering and wondered if we could pick him up and get him out of there. We took Scott to our home and visited with him for four or five hours. He seemed to be a genuine Christian and was very amiable. It was as if he was part of the family. He even acted like an older brother to our young children.

When it came time to leave for the campaign, Scott suggested that due to the stress of the last several days and his leg being in a fresh cast that he would rather stay home and get some rest. He volunteered to watch our children if we wanted to leave them. We agreed and told him we'd be home in two hours. Debbie and I felt totally at ease with our new-found Christian friend. We left Scott in charge of our children, ages three, five, and six years old.

That particular night, it was Debbie's turn to lead worship and Arturo's turn to preach. I would attend to help minister in prayer at the end of the service. We were in the car and had traveled about one hundred yards when something happened that I will never, ever forget. The Holy Spirit spoke in a *very loud voice* directly into my heart. *How do you know this man isn't a pedophile?*

The overwhelming force of that question hit me like a sledgehammer. I stopped the car immediately in the middle of traffic.

I turned and said to Debbie, "I forgot I need to call someone. It's very important. I have to go back to the house. Maybe I'll see you later at the campaign. If not, I'll see you back at home."

She accepted my impromptu lie and drove on to the campaign without me. I couldn't tell her what I'd just heard. I had to get home, quick.

I arrived less than two minutes after I had left, and everything was fine. The kids were playing quietly, and Scott was in the living room. After I was home for less than a minute, the phone rang. It was the hospital where Scott stayed. They informed me that Scott had *not* been attacked by thieves. He had attempted suicide. That was the reason for the broken leg. Furthermore, they reported that he had AIDS, and we should be careful with our contact with him. A minute after I hung up, the phone rang again. This time it was the U.S. Embassy in Quito. It was the second in command at the consulate. He said they knew Scott had AIDS and that he was at our house. Since it was 1990, the AIDS epidemic was new and much was still unknown about the deadly disease. The Embassy asked us to help them get Scott back to the United States as soon as possible.

He said, "This will be an international embarrassment if it hits the Ecuadorian Press."

I agreed to help and met him at the Embassy the next day to start Scott's evacuation. They agreed to pay for the return ticket and assist with the paper work.

When I confronted Scott, he hung his head and admitted that he did have AIDS. He confessed that he lied about the thieves instead of coming clean about his suicide attempt. I forgave him and told him that the United States Embassy wanted him out of the country quickly. He spent the night. Early the next day, we scrambled to get him back to the States.

We ran around all day and got the paperwork in order for his rapid departure. We also had to get the money from the Embassy and buy his return ticket. We got back to the house late in the afternoon to get ready for his departure early the next day.

After I had been home a few minutes, one of my children came to me and said, "Daddy, Scott showed me something."

"What did he show you?" I asked.

"I don't know, but there were naked people in the pictures."

That got my attention, and Debbie's too. We further questioned our child.

I got Scott alone and read him the riot act.

"What have you done with my child?" I demanded.

Scott said, "Nothing, I just showed a few pictures."

I soon found the pornographic photos in his suitcase and kicked him out of the house.

"If I weren't a Christian, I would have easily thrown you out the third-story window without a second thought."

I was furious and scared about what had just happened to my child. Now, I fully understood what the Holy Spirit shouted into my heart the day before.

Scott was on the plane the next morning, and I never heard from him again. I was concerned about how this pornographic exposure affected my child. I prayed. I asked questions numerous times over the ensuing months and years. Everything was confusing and hazy. Ten years later, while walking to school with a friend, a stranger inappropriately touched their stomach while crossing the street. This brought back a flood of deeply buried memories of that awful event years earlier. It was like a movie being played in their mind causing them to feel dirty, violated, and fearful. My teenager wouldn't leave their room for two days, until I returned from the jungle to Quito. Now, we understood the depth and seriousness of what happed ten years prior with that pedophile, Scott.

A good friend of mine, missionary Jim DeGloyer, who knew about the event and the trauma now upon my child, asked if I wanted to pray with him for healing. He introduced me to the Theophostic Prayer Ministry, by Dr. Edward Smith, a Christian Psychologist. It focuses on bringing the light, truth, and perspective of Christ to take the place of lie-based memories that happened through traumatic experiences. It is a prayer dialogue that allows the wounded person to have a divine encounter with the living Christ, who transmits healing and liberty as His Truth enters the deepest recesses of their spirit (John 8:32,36).

As we prayed with my sixteen-year-old, Jim said, "If Jesus says or communicates anything to you, please tell us. So we know how to keep praying."

Shortly into the prayer session, my teenager said, "Dad, Jesus was with me. He told me to go to you and mom when Scott threatened me and told me not to tell you about the pictures." This was an important revelation to my child, because they thought Jesus abandoned them during this horrible situation.

We kept praying.

After a few more minutes, my child said, "Jesus just told me that my experience was like a little scratch compared to what happens to many children who suffer abuse for many years."

"Wow," I said, "that's incredible."

Jim and I kept praying.

Soon, my teenager said to us, "Jesus just took His hand and ran it across the memory in my mind. He completely erased it, Dad. Jesus just totally erased all those tormenting and filthy memories. I can't see them anymore."

The memories never returned.

Jim and I were stunned beyond words. Yet, here was my child proclaiming, with tears of joy, freedom from all the pornographic memories of ten years prior. I never experienced this kind of miracle before.

This experience shaped and guided a major part of my ministry in Ecuador Teen Challenge, my seminary classes and prayer ministry. I can clearly see now that *ALL things work together for good to those who love God, to those who are called according to His Purpose* (Romans 8:28). I never would have involved myself in this mind-transforming ministry if it wasn't for what God allowed to happen to my child many years ago. My child even began to minister to many hurting young people this same grace from Jesus. (If you are interested in knowing more about Theophostic Prayer, go to Dr. Smith's website: www.Theophostic.com)

Chapter 26

Danger in the Mountains and Rivers

―――――◇◆◇――――――

It was April 2013. I took my motorcycle up the eight-mile, winding, dirt road on Pichincha Mountain. I got up there about 11:00 a.m. that Saturday morning and chained my motorcycle to a fence near the radio antennas. I made the same trip countless times in the previous twenty-six years to pray and enjoy God's incredible beauty overlooking the city of Quito. There was wonderful solitude and peace at the 15,000 foot altitude. The hustle and bustle of the two million people below seemed so far away and unable to touch me in those celestial airs.

I took my five children up there to hike, repel off the cliffs, and even camp out as they grew up in Ecuador. All of them loved its beauty and majesty as much as I did. Every time they returned to Ecuador to visit, they hiked up and enjoyed the pure air and freedom that Pichincha offered.

According to several guide books about Ecuador, anyone visiting Quito should be aware of the danger of thieves that might assault you on the high and desolate Pichincha Mountain. I met people who had this terrible experience and heard many horror stories. Radio station technicians and tourists were robbed, stripped of their clothes, and made to spend the night up there in the dark.

I never had any such experiences, nor had my children. But that was about to change.

I decided to climb both mountains leading up to my prayer spot that I called The Condor's Nest. It was situated high above a great ravine overlooking the city. It was a perfect place to pray, worship, and commune with God. I could be absolutely alone there. I had never encountered anyone at that spot in close to thirty years.

I skirted around the first large hill and climbed the first of two mountains. I felt an unusual alertness in my spirit, more than usual. As I came down the first mountain, I noticed movement high up the second mountain near the Condor's Nest. It looked like several people moving around up on the high grassy top of the mountain. I couldn't be sure. It was still close to a mile away. I came all the way down the first mountain, crossed the several hundred yards of the valley and began my ascent to the Condor's Nest. I was still wondering about the flurry of activity I'd just seen. I felt uneasy inside. At the half-way point up the second mountain, I stopped to get a drink of water from my backpack. I stood there for about ten minutes and looked for any sign of activity at the top of the mountain. I'm glad I did.

All of a sudden, five men rushed out from hiding in the tall grass on top of the mountain. They descended rapidly and headed in my direction. With about four hundred yards between us, I had to make a quick decision. The scripture from Proverbs 22:3 came to mind powerfully. *A prudent man foresees evil and hides himself, but the simple pass on and are punished.*

I said, "Lord, I want to be a prudent man and hide myself."

The four hundred yards and the 15,000-foot altitude worked in my favor and I needed to use it. If I had continued up the mountain, I would have been right in front of them. Instead, I was four hundred yards below them when they decided to come after me. God had stopped me in my tracks. He knew I needed that distance to escape. He wasn't surprised at all by their tactics.

I turned around and walked quickly, but not too quickly. If I moved too fast at that altitude I would have to stop to recover from oxygen deprivation and muscle fatigue. That would allow the thieves to catch up with me. I had to keep my pace not too fast and not too slow. That required a huge amount of concentration and self-control as I imagined them closing in on me.

When I reached the second mountain, I took the hidden path that allowed me to go around instead of up. I knew this area very well but maybe they didn't. I was still at least two miles from the place my motorcycle was chained. The entire distance was desolate until I reached the radio antennas. As I came around the second mountain, I allowed myself the first look behind me since I set out thirty minutes earlier. There was no one. They hadn't found the hidden path. My shortcut gave me the incredible break I needed to escape and stay hidden from view. I was ecstatic. The Holy Spirit warned me in my heart about their evil plan and helped me escape when it looked impossible.

I have returned to hike and pray there, many times, as before. I am always alert but confident that God will continue to protect me as I seek His Face. I do not presume safety or take anything for granted. However, I will not let the enemy keep me from my appointed meetings with the Lord.

> *Surely He shall deliver you from the snare of the*
> *fowler and from the perilous pestilence. He shall*
> *cover you with His feathers, and under His wings*
> *you shall take refuge (Psalm 91:3-4).*

Danger in the River

My sons, Derek and Philip, reminded me about the Christmas we spent in the village of Kusutka several years ago. We gave the children small bags of cookies and candies, called *navidenos*, at the evening church service. The next day, we planned to hike three hours to the village of Mamayac, cross the Pastaza River, hike three more hours to the village of Chapintza, and catch a bus out of the jungle.

Instead, when we arrived in Mamayac, the villagers told us to hike another hour up to Karink Village and cross there. It was too dangerous to cross in Mamayac because of the swift current and flooding caused by recent rains. We pressed on and arrived an hour later in Karink, where we discovered that the 30-foot canoe needed to cross the river was parked 250 yards away on the other side. We called out for whoever used the canoe and spent thirty minutes waiting for them to return. No one came.

Derek said to his brother, "Come on, let's swim it."

I cringed inside. Both of my sons were in the best physical condition of their lives and excellent swimmers, but the Pastaza River was a monster. That day, there were whirlpools, a 12-mile-per-hour current, and two- to three-foot waves in the middle of the river. I remained on shore with our 30-year-old Shuar Guide, Ivan.

I grabbed ahold of Ivan's hand, and said, "We're going to pray until they are safely on the other side."

They hiked almost 500 yards upstream to compensate for the powerful current and dove in. Their arms stroked through the water with purpose and power. Yet, within moments, they were carried by the current past Ivan and me. They swam together until they reached the middle of the river. Their struggle intensified as they battled the downward pull of the whirlpools and the even-faster current. Philip bumped into Derek. That bump separated them. I started really worrying. I couldn't do anything to help them, and now they didn't even have each other.

Ivan and I continued to cry out to God for their safety. Finally, Derek reached the small beach on the other side. Philip made it to shore, seconds behind him, just before the beach ended. They were so exhausted that they didn't move for about fifteen minutes. The funny ending to this story was the "Full Moon" Derek gave the whole jungle. His shorts fell to his ankles during the swim, and he didn't even have the energy to pull them up once he made it to the beach.

Ivan said, "No one has *ever* swam across the river at this village." Now, Derek and Philip are part of Shuar Indian lore, because it will probably never happen again. God answered prayer and showed His mercy in the Pastaza river crossing.

Chapter 27

The Clouds Departed

⟶———————⟨⟩⟨⟩———————⟵

I t was November 2006. The church planting project in South
Quito was going well with Pastor Edgar Naranjo and his wife
Elsa, or so we thought. With the help of several churches, we
bought property for a 400-person church. Plans for the new
building also included Sunday School accommodations, youth
rooms, and administration offices. My construction foreman,
Oswaldo, worked tirelessly for several months to get the metal
roof on the building before the arrival of the first of three construction teams from the States. He succeeded in getting the
main beams in place and many of the support beams. However,
the roof wouldn't be in place until after Pastor Jerry Terry and
the first team were scheduled to leave Ecuador. We certainly
wanted to put this large group of volunteers to good use. The
group was made up of twenty-five people from Calvary's Love
and twenty people from Pastor Edgar's church. We had forty-
five able bodies who were eager to work.

Since the roof wasn't done, we would make the best of it and
pour the cement floor without it. That isn't a problem if it isn't

raining. The problem was, we were entering the rainy season when the team arrived.

It took a couple days to get all the wooden forms built and in place. On the third day, we had two portable cement mixers running to keep all forty-five people busy. By midday, we had poured several truckloads of cement and were making wonderful progress. Then we felt raindrops.

Oh no! I thought. *This cannot be happening.*

All the wet cement was exposed to the rain. There was no way to cover it or prevent it from getting rained on. More than half the floor was already poured, and it would be ruined if the rain fell on it now.

I quickly gathered about eight people to join me in the storage shed. We fell on our knees and prayed for a miracle. Then we prayed some more. Five minutes went by, then ten. Some people left. *But it was still raining.* We prayed and cried out for a miracle to stop the rain. After fifteen minutes it slowed. After twenty minutes it *completely* stopped. To our utter joy and amazement, we went outside and saw a large blue hole in the clouds. All around us, it was raining buckets. However, directly above us the clouds parted, and we had blue skies. It stayed that way for the rest of the week. We continued to pour the floor, stairs and walkways on the church with no roof. We didn't have another drop of rain. Our God is a miracle-working God.

So the men marveled, saying, "Who can this be, that even the winds and the sea obey Him?"
(Matthew 8:27).

Chapter 28

Brought Back to Life

————————◇×◇————————

In 1990, Debbie and I started our first work in Quito, Ecuador. It was a tent campaign that went non-stop seven nights a week for two years. During that time, we had exciting and interesting things happen. Dogs, drunks, and curious people often wandered into the tent to see the "circus." One particular evening, Youth Pastor Galo Benites was preaching.

A drunk stood up on the front row of seats and proclaimed, "You're a voice crying out in the wilderness."

Another time, Debbie led worship in the tent when a drunk worked his way to the front and up onto the platform. He was ready to take the microphone out of Debbie's hand when two of our Ecuadorian leaders stepped in and stopped him. They politely escorted him off the stage.

One night, however, was very different. A visiting evangelist preached that night. We just came to the end of the service and finished the altar call. Pastor Arturo was closing the service when a neighbor from across the street came into the tent with her two-year-old son. The child was lifeless in her arms.

The woman was not a Christian and had never attended any of our services.

Evidently, her toddler had been playing on the ten-foot cement wall that bordered her house. The child fell head first onto the street. She took him to several other neighbors who owned businesses but was turned away. Now, she was here in our tent pleading for help.

The evangelist immediately took the child into his arms and prayed. Soon, many of the remaining Christians joined him. After several minutes, we noticed that the child's eyes moved. Then his head moved to the side. Soon, he began to cry. He came back. He was not breathing when she brought him in. Everyone saw that for sure. The other neighbors turned her away, because they didn't want the responsibility of paying for a funeral for her child. Now, everything was different. He was alive again. Wow. That had a huge impact on the faith of the many new believers at the tent campaign.

> *I am He who lives, and was dead, and behold, I am alive forevermore. Amen. And I have the **keys of Hades and of Death***
> (Revelation 1:18, emphasis added).

Chapter 29

The Power of Prayer

————————◇※◇————————

This very interesting and entertaining story of faith is about my good friend Jorge Ailla. He co-founded Ecuador Teen Challenge with me. We also work together in the jungle with the Shuar Indians.

Jorge ministered in the jungle several years ago in the Pastaza Province of Ecuador. He noticed over the course of several days that he wasn't feeling well. When he finally returned to Quito he couldn't even stand up or walk. He suffered from a condition known as thrombosis in his legs. It slowed his blood flow almost to a standstill. He managed to get to the hospital in the city of Ambato but was all alone and without any money. The hospital took him in and agreed he could repay them later. Jorge was there for three days. The doctors told him that many times his condition was fatal or amputation of the affected limbs was required. Overwhelmed by his circumstances, he felt sorry for himself and didn't know what to do.

As he wallowed in self-pity the Holy Spirit spoke to him. *Jorge, what are you doing just lying there? Get up and start praying for people worse off than you.* He knew he was being challenged.

Jorge got out of bed and waddled to the person in the bed next to him. He started praying. At the time, he was hooked up to two IVs that he rolled around with him. Soon, he was praying with doctors, nurses and all the patients on his floor. Many people came to Christ. The more he prayed the better he felt. Within two weeks he made a remarkable recovery. He came back to Quito a new man … a victorious man.

Jorge testifies, "It was the best thing that could have happened to me. God used my infirmity to draw me closer to Him and show His Glory to others."

A year later, Jorge was back in Quito when he fell ill with a terrible virus that he just couldn't shake. For several weeks he pushed through the discomfort but grew weaker. Early Saturday morning was prayer time for the church. Several families and their children gathered with Jorge at 5:00 a.m. to pray. All Jorge could do was lie there and cry out to God.

He yelled over to the young children, "Come over and lay your hands on me and pray."

They did. About eight children cried out for God to heal their pastor. With tears in their eyes and fire in their hearts they prayed and prayed. After about twenty minutes, a great power came into Jorge's body. He felt strength and healing flow into him like a mighty river.

He stood on his feet and proclaimed, "I am healed."

And he was.

Jorge has since brought these young children into the jungle with him and encouraged them to minister to the Shuar children. Miracles of healing and evangelism are coming from these little ones who just believe God.

Pray for one another, that you may be healed
(James 5:16).

And a little child shall lead them (Isaiah 11:6).

Chapter 30

Robbers Thwarted

—✧✦✧—

This final chapter is about two very interesting events that happened to a friend of mine. His name is Diego Ushina. Diego has lived in the jungle village of Kusutka with his family for the last ten years. He has many stories of faith and adventure that he could share. I have the privilege of sharing two of them within the pages of this book.

In April of 2009, Diego and his family had lived in the deep jungle for four years. His oldest son Samuel told Diego that he really wanted some meat to eat, since it had been so long. Diego prayed with his son for this request. It was 11:00 p.m.

Samuel replied, "I know Jesus heard me, daddy. I'm going to bed."

In his heart Diego felt terrible because they were out of food and had no money to buy any. They couldn't even afford to leave the jungle. He felt like he wasn't a good provider for his family. It was a restless night for Diego.

At 4:00 a.m. the next morning, there came a knock on the door. It was a man from the San Francisco village, about a five-hour hike from Kusutka. He came in with several pounds of fresh meat.

The man said, "My cow died all of a sudden last night. I don't know why. She was a good and healthy cow. Anyway, here is some meat from her."

Diego immediately woke up Samuel. "Here is the meat you prayed for."

"I know, daddy. Jesus let me know He would get it for me. I'm going back to sleep. It's *so* early."

As you can see, it took exactly the amount of time from the prayer until the man knocked on the door to walk the distance through the jungle in the dark. In addition to the perfect timing, to walk through the jungle in the dark is a very unusual thing to do.

For the rest of that month, food came in from all sides in great abundance. What an awesome God we serve.

> *I have been young, and now am old; Yet I have not seen the righteous forsaken, nor his descendants begging bread* (Psalm 37:25).

Diego's second story is about a time he and his youngest son Daniel traveled by bus between Macas and Puyo in November of 2013. The Holy Spirit told him that there was a thief on the bus. In fact, there were several thieves. They planned to carry out their plot where there was no cell phone coverage between the two towns about an hour into the ride.

Diego went up to the bus driver and said, "There is a thief on this bus."

The man looked at Diego in unbelief.

A women overheard Diego talking to the bus driver.

"Yes, he's right," she said. "I just had my cell phone stolen. I can't find it anywhere."

Diego noticed a man giving him the evil eye.

"That's the thief!" proclaimed Diego.

Just then, two out-of-uniform policemen woke up. They were passengers sitting in the front of the bus and were startled by the commotion.

Diego repeated, "That man is a thief."

"No I am not," replied the man loudly.

"If you're not," responded the policeman, "why are you staring with such hate in your eyes at this man?"

Diego suggested that the policemen have everyone get off the bus with their belongings and search the bus. They did and found several large sacks with knives and the woman's cell phone. Upon further investigation, they phoned in the suspected man's social security number and discovered his long record of armed robberies. They called a patrol car and hauled him off to jail.

When the bus continued on in its journey, Diego noticed a red car waiting exactly where there was no cell phone coverage. A single man got off at that location. He was the second thief thwarted by the Holy Spirit's intervention. God was so good to His servant, Diego, his son Daniel and all the people on the bus that night.

> *Mark the blameless man, and observe the upright;*
> *for the future of that man is peace. But the trans-*
> *gressors shall be destroyed together; the future of the*
> *wicked shall be cut off* (Psalm 37:37-38).

Epilogue

W ell, it's May 2016, and the thirty stories have been written. These were only highlights. There are many more to tell. Lord willing, we will continue to serve the Lord here in Ecuador for years to come. The Ecuador Teen Challenge is doing well with our wonderful staff to help me run it. The jungle churches and schools continue to thrive and multiply. We are now expanding our seminary extension and are expecting forty students from both provinces this coming year. The Holy Spirit Conferences in the Pastaza and Morona Santiago Provinces had 1,200 participants with forty villages represented last year. It is truly a time of harvest.

The last thought that I'd like to leave with you is this: God really does show up. When we get ourselves into troubles or things are completely out of our control, keep continually looking up. He is in the midst of the storms and whirlwinds of life. When you've gone through several of these experiences with Jesus, your trust will be more established, and you will truly believe *that **all** things work together for **good** to those who love God, to those who are the called according to His purpose* (Romans 8:28, emphasis added).

Now to Him who is able to keep you from stumbling,
and to present you faultless before the presence of
His glory with exceeding joy, to God our Savior, who
alone is wise, be glory and majesty, dominion and
power, both now and forever. Amen (Jude 24-25).

Let us finish STRONG the race that God has called us to run. And let us live and be willing to die for the words of Jesus that proclaim, *Well done, good and faithful servant; ... enter into the joy of your Lord.* (Matthew 25:23).

A Prayer to Receive Christ

The whole purpose for writing *30 Stories in 30 Years* is to glorify God and demonstrate how ready and willing He is to help us at any time. I would be remiss if I did not include a final prayer for those who want to know this God of mine, who has been so faithful to me all these years. He is ready to receive us into His arms, forgive us of all our sins, and welcome us into His Eternal Kingdom. If you want this, pray with me:

I come to you, Heavenly Father, just as I am. I rec-
ognize my need of you. I ask for forgiveness of all my
sins through the name of your Son, Jesus Christ. I
receive His shed blood as payment for all I've done
wrong. Come into my heart, Holy Spirit, and lead
me to all truth. I receive Your light in exchange for
my darkness. Thank you for leading me in Your
path, and safely guiding me throughout my life to be
able to enter your Eternal Kingdom, to live with You
forever! Amen.

Praying this prayer of salvation out loud is the first, very important step in following Jesus. (Romans 10:9, 10) It is the most important thing that we can do in this life. If you have just done this, please write us on our Facebook link and let me know. I would love to hear from you.

If you want to keep up with our continuing ministry in Ecuador, go to our Facebook page: www.facebook.com/ecuadorecho

About the Author

Tim grew up in Baldwinsville, NY. He was a three-sport athlete in high school, (soccer, track, and gymnastics) and a member of the Ivy League Championship Gymnastics Team of Cornell University in 1976 and '77. Tim came to a relationship with Christ in 1975 due to the testimony and influence of his mother, Kathleen. He left his banking career to live and minister at Syracuse Teen Challenge and Syracuse Rescue Mission from 1979 through 1985. Tim and his wife Debbie were appointed AGWM missionaries in 1986 and have served in Ecuador since that time. Their ministry includes: Founding and Directing Ecuador Teen Challenge, planting churches in Quito and the jungle, directing four Christian Schools in the jungle with more than 400 students, and teaching in the Quito and Riobamba Seminaries.

Connect with Tim

https://www.facebook.com/ecuadorecho/

If you would like to support us monthly or give a one-time gift, then go to: giving.ag.org, enter #224040, and click search. You'll find Timothy H. Anderson, Ecuador.

American bush pilot Russell Stendal, on routine business, landed his plane in a remote Colombian village. Gunfire exploded throughout the town, and within minutes Russell's 142-day ordeal had begun. The Colombian cartel explained that this was a kidnapping for ransom and that he would be held until payment was made.

Held at gunpoint deep in the jungle and with little else to occupy his time, Russell asked for some paper and began to write. He told the story of his life and kept a record of his experience in the guerrilla camp. His "book" became a bridge to the men who held him hostage and now serves as the basis for this incredible true story of how God's love penetrated a physical and ideological jungle.

To buy *Rescue the Captors*, visit www.anekopress.com:

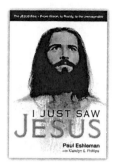

This miraculous story reveals how *JESUS* began as one man's vision and became a record-breaking film shown more than 9 billion times and convincing millions to follow Christ.

Volunteer film teams, missionaries, and pastors risk their lives daily, showing the film in remote tribes and villages, among religions that strictly prohibit Christianity, and even to the world's most elite and powerful leaders. They have overcome threats, witches' curses, and deadly diseases. The teams carry compact generators and portable projectors, often traveling by foot or horseback, bush plane or canoe. Their pure, unbridled joy comes from sharing *JESUS* with those who have not yet seen and heard the gospel.

The story behind the film that:

- Has been seen more than 9 billion times.
- Is in the *Guinness World Records* for most translated film ever.
- Results in thirty to fifty thousand indicating a desire to follow Jesus every day.

To buy *I Just Saw Jesus*, visit www.anekopress.com:

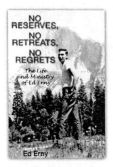

My life story begins with a preacher who, by the leading of the Spirit, refused to end a service until my father, a successful businessman, had given his heart to the Lord. I eventually followed in my father's footsteps into full-time ministry, but only after overcoming self-doubt and self-consciousness in my ability to share the gospel.

God took that doubt away when a young man gave his heart to the Lord after I told him about Jesus. From that moment on, in Taiwan, the Philippines, and other places where I served, I saw the tremendous hand of the Lord at work as I allowed Him to lead and work through me. My desire is that you will be inspired and motivated to serve the Lord as freely and willingly as I was privileged to do for many years. May you, by God's grace, determine to live with no reserves, no retreats, and no regrets.

To buy *No Reserves, No Retreats, No Regrets*, visit www.anekopress.com:

In its early years, Duluth was a gold mine for lumber barons. Men were employed as lumberjacks and worked like beasts, only to be tossed aside like used equipment when no longer needed. The grand forests were raped for their prime timber, the balance burned wastefully. The men were coarse and hard, but they had to be to survive. More than any other people that ever lived in our land, these old-time lumberjacks could truthfully say, "No man cared for my soul."

That is, until God sent three men to the great Northwoods of our country – Frank Higgins, John Sornberger, and Al Channer. These men blazed new trails of the Spirit and founded an empire for God. They reached a sector of humanity for which no spiritual work had ever been done before, storming the Northwoods with a consuming passion for Christ. And with that passion, they also brought a heart as big as all outdoors, a love for men that burned like a flame, and a desperate desire to see these men saved.

To buy *The Last of the Giants*, visit www.anekopress.com:

CPSIA information can be obtained
at www.ICGtesting.com
Printed in the USA
FFOW03n1543161116
29434FF